"Thank you, Kelly, fo   MW01491743
this book. Abortion is a .... that doesn't go away completely, but each day that we allow Jesus to forgive and love us, we heal
more and more. This book is a must-read for those living with guilt
and shame and who need a guide to experience freedom and healing."

Jon Gordon,
Positive Mindset Coach and Author of thirty books,
including seventeen best sellers and five children's books

One in every four women carry the heartbreak of abortion—often in
secret, often for a lifetime, often believing God could never forgive
them. In *The Soul's Hole*, Kelly Proehl helps us see that no matter the
reason a woman decides to end a pregnancy, the mental, emotional,
physical, and spiritual impact is rarely expected but very real. The heavy
weight of guilt, regret, shame and grief tear the threads of her soul.

Vulnerably confessing a time in her twenties when she "wanted
the uncertainty of the ordeal over, the recovery done, and everything forgotten," Kelly shares a secret that would be easier to keep
because she longs for women to know—they are not alone, and
they are worth the fight for healing and freedom! With unfiltered
honesty, deep compassion and a gentle yet bold spirit, Kelly guides
hurting women to bring their brokenness to Jesus so they can find
forgiveness and peace! Kelly's story will give you courage to face
the past and find a future filled with "a love that penetrates to your
deepest fears and heals your shame—a love that will not let you go!"

Renee Swope,
best-selling author of A Confident Heart

"Transparent, painful, powerful, and full of hope. Kelly cou-
rageously invites you to walk with her through the pain of her
abortion experience so that she might point you to the glorious
forgiveness, healing, and hope available in Christ. She writes with
a tender truthfulness that disarms, informs, and inspires. Whether
you have your own experience with abortion or desire to minister
to those who do, you will be helped as you follow Kelly through
her experience and unto her Savior."

Pastor Clint Darst /
King's Cross Church, Greensboro, North Carolina

Kelly's courageous journey is a gift to anyone who has ever carried silent pain, wrestled with an impossible decision, or feared that their story was beyond redemption. I deeply admire and respect Kelly for her willingness to revisit a painful season of her life, not for attention or sympathy, but to offer compassion, clarity, and hope for others.

Abortion is a profoundly complex issue. It is often wrapped in fear, shame, confusion, and grief, and far too many walk through it alone. Kelly speaks to that silence with honesty, tenderness, and tremendous bravery. Her words remind us that even in our darkest chapters, God is present and redemption is possible. She does not simplify or diminish the emotions involved; instead, she brings perspective, empathy, and the reassurance that healing and restoration can find us right where we are.

Kelly's story is one of truth-telling and grace. It is filled with hope and life. I am grateful for her voice, her vulnerability, and her willingness to show that beauty can emerge from a place of pain.

Kathrine Lee,
Founder & CEO, Pure Hope Foundation

"Kelly has written her story with vulnerability, always leading the reader into the arms of Christ. It is never easy to share our abortion experiences whether we've had one or five abortions. A stigma and fear of condemnation keeps us silent, yet most people have a great deal of compassion for the woundedness of our hearts once they know the truth. Kelly draws the reader into her story with simplicity—encouraging and equipping the reader to want to take the next step in healing with song suggestions, scripture, healing resources, and through the transparency of her own healing journey. This book is for anyone at any stage in their healing journey."

Mindy Lefaucheur,
Founder and President, "An Even Place,"
Abortion Recovery Virtual Healing Groups

THE SOUL'S HOLE

LIVING IN FREEDOM & JOY AFTER ABORTION

MY HEALING STORY

KELLY BAKER PROEHL

Made for Success Publishing
www.MadeForSuccess.com

Distributed by Made for Success Publishing

First Printing

Library of Congress Cataloging-in-Publication data
Proehl, Kelly
    The Soul's Hole: Living in Freedom and Joy After Abortion p. cm.

    LCCN: 2025948702
    ISBN: 978-1-64146-973-9 *(Paperback)*
    ISBN: 978-1-64146-974-6 *(eBook)*
    ISBN: 978-1-64146-975-3 *(Audio)*

Printed in the United States of America

For further information, contact Made for Success Publishing
email service@madeforsuccess.net

for the one who will walk with me to the Cross

for healing and freedom

THE CHAPTERS OF MY STORY

SPECIAL THANKS

IT WAS VERY clear to me that the Lord was asking me to write this book. But when I considered the extreme vulnerability it would take, and how abortion always involves others, I wrestled with it. When I finally surrendered to the idea, I needed to ask those I love the most if they were okay with it because it would expose them as well. To my surprise, they weren't just okay; they encouraged me to do it.

Thank you to my Jersey boy—my husband and best friend, Ricky, for your on-the-daily transparency. With you, it's always been "you see what you get." Many of those rough edges have smoothed out as your walk with Jesus has deepened. Your legacy will always be true faith because you always point us back to believing, not when things are easy, but when things are upside-down. Thank you for always making me laugh and for the life we have lived together. It's been an incredible adventure! Thumbs out.

Thank you to our precious living children, Alex, Austin, and Blake. Being your mom and watching you grow up are among the greatest joys of my life. We didn't deserve you, but God, in His mercy, gave the three of you to us. You each have such beautiful talents that are making an impact for God's Kingdom. Never stop.

To my parents, where my heart has always been "home." I have always loved spending time with you, and that never changes. The way you love others, live in generosity, and love God has forever shaped me.

Thank you *all* for loving the Lord so much that you wanted others to hear our story. The most beautiful part of it is that you all know it's not really our story; we know it's Jesus' story, and He is the hero in it.

Thank you to one of my best friends from college, Julie Ann, who was the first to read an early, very messy draft of this book. You are a precious gift from God. As close as we were in college, I chose not to tell you or any of our close college friends about my abortion. When I finally did, many years later, you loved me with Christ's love.

As a gifted writer yourself, thank you for being willing to challenge me while writing this book, helping me believe in myself, and helping me tap into more senses in my story. You are kind, giving, smart, and a blessing to me. I am forever grateful that the Lord brought us together in college and that our friendship has endured many years and seasons of life.

I have very close sisters in Jesus who have prayed for me while writing this book, especially during the warfare. With my whole heart, I thank God for each of you. There is no greater treasure than living alongside you, who are always ready to praise Jesus, pray for one another, laugh and cry together, and celebrate each other as women.

Amy, Leigh, Jacquie, Keyah, Teresa, and Mindy, you all inspire me. Because of women like you, who are brave enough to bring their stories into the light, I am stronger, and other women will be, too. Thank you for allowing your stories to be in this book.

Thank you to our pastor, Clint Darst, for making sure I stayed theologically faithful in my writing and encouraging me in this journey.

To Renee, who God used to help me pull up my big girl pants and get back to writing. You have mentored me as an author yourself and held me accountable. I do not doubt that that day in the airport was divinely orchestrated. I am grateful for you.

To our two beloved children in heaven, Sweet Angel and Brooklyn, we will all meet you one day, and we will dance, play, and rejoice being together forever in heaven! There will never be any separation again. Thank you Father.

And lastly, but always mostly, Jesus. You are Holy, yet so extremely gentle and kind. You drew me to Yourself in my filth. You didn't have to do that, but that's who You are. You are my everything.

WHY

NEVER, IN A million years, did I think that I would be writing a book, or that this would be my story. I grew up a homebody, and I wasn't the cool girl. People thought I was a "goody-goody." During my senior year of high school, I could be found at home on Friday nights with my parents and my boyfriend, eating Krispy Kreme™ doughnuts and watching television. I didn't party before going to college. Yet four years after graduating high school, I had an abortion.

There have been more days than not that I have wanted to delete every word of this book and ignore the pressing on my heart to write it. It is a dark, shameful part of my life that would be much easier to keep a secret. Although I feel that I will live forever with a hole of regret in my soul from this choice, I want to share how God rescued and healed me. Even more, I *need* to share.

We do not talk enough about women who are living in spiritual, emotional, physical, and mental bondage from abortion. When a woman starts thinking about abortion, then walks into an abortion clinic, it's game on—the spiritual battle is raging.

Our healing is no different. We must contend for our healing. When we have the courage to face the truth, choose to heal, and eventually share our story with others, we see how it helps others open up and heal. I've seen it again and again. This is how God uses community to heal us. Denial will never lead to freedom. We can't heal what we don't admit, and we can't overcome what we don't acknowledge.

I believe, with all that I am, that we are all broken and need a Healer, post-abortive or not. We all have a void in our souls that can only be filled and healed with the identity and peace of Jesus Christ. If it's not Jesus, whatever fills that void will be temporary. Jesus is forever. Our souls search for identity, freedom, and rest, which are found in Jesus. We are restless until we surrender our lives to Him. I hope that, whether you believe that or not, you will still read my story with an open heart.

In my post-abortive experience, that hole (or wound) has been healed by Jesus with forgiveness, freedom, joy, and peace ... even abundant life; however, once I woke up to the truth of my abortion, I found that a hole in my soul remained in memory of the child. It's not that the wound hasn't healed, but the regret and grief are lifelong—or at least, it is proving that way for me. I live in sadness, yet also, in freedom, simultaneously, proving there are always consequences for our decisions—good or bad.

My guess, if you are holding this book, you are more than likely the one out of every four women who has experienced abortion(s) and walked into one of the coldest, most lifeless four walls that exist: an abortion center. If you're not one of those women, maybe you took a friend, sat with a friend, or know a friend who has been there. Look around the church pews, the grocery line, the treadmills at the gym, your class reunion, the bus seats, your Bible study group, the conference room, the restaurant tables ... one in four women. That's a lot of women.

Many of them never share their story with anyone in their entire life. I hope that you read this book and feel community not only from my story, but also from the other women who share theirs. Like me, they bare their souls; one was even raped and chose life. I want you to know that if you made this choice, you are not alone.

This is a digging-in journey, but I know you are ready because you are holding this book. This is a huge first step, and I am proud of you.

Whatever your reason for reading my story, remember it is not a coincidence or an accident. What's kept in the dark can never heal. God is pursuing you at this very moment, but an enemy after your soul doesn't want you to believe that. Don't let the enemy win. You are worth the fight that will bring peace to your soul.

So, what led this homebody and "goody-goody" to make such a decision? Who was I at that time in my life to decide abortion was the solution? How did God pursue me, and how did I respond so He could heal me? How do I now live the abundant life He desires for each of us? I want to share my story with you—soul-exposed, heart-wide-open—because I yearn for you to find freedom and joy, as I have. I yearn for you to know the Jesus who wants to carry you and heal your grief, shame, and guilt. I have no other reason for writing this book.

Come on this journey with me.

1 / *white lace*

OUT ON THE country roads on the outskirts of Raleigh, North Carolina, I grew up riding my go-cart around the neighborhood, pretending like each driveway was a new road to a different city in the world. If I was driving, I'd have one of my sisters—Kim or Kristi—or a neighborhood friend as my co-pilot. I loved swinging from trees on rope swings. I loved sledding down the steep, snow-covered hill by the tennis courts. In the spring and summer, I loved playing by the creek, catching crawfish, and making forts. I loved playing hopscotch in my driveway. I loved pretending to be the teacher and teaching school to my neighborhood friends. I also loved pretending I was Olivia Newton-John in Grease and singing "You Better Shape Up" with my sisters. I loved singing opera and dancing all over the house. All in all, I remember having a very happy, loving childhood. My mom stayed home to raise us, and my dad worked at our family roofing business.

As I grew older, I tried sports, but that quickly ended when I got walloped in the stomach with a soccer ball. I lost my breath and thought I was going to die.

My sports career was short-lived, except for some cheerleading later in high school and college. I also tried some theatre and ballet, but I mostly loved to spend time with my small friend group, at the beach on my Sunfish sailboat, taking horseback riding lessons, or at home with my parents.

School was always important to me. I valued doing well in my classes and getting good grades.

What kind of little girl were you? Were we similar? Were you more of the girly type who loved to dress up in your mom's heels and dresses? Or maybe you were neither a tomboy nor a girly girl. Maybe you liked reading. Maybe you loved shooting hoops and kicking balls. Maybe you just tried to survive. I believe we all start so innocent, so pure. No matter what we were like back then, we inherently craved love and protection. We deserved that, but life-happened—broken people happened. Then we made choices in our own brokenness, and our lives became an accumulation of it all.

As I shared, I grew up in a loving home with both parents present, and they are incredible people.

My mom is truly one of the sweetest people I know. People are drawn to her because of her warmth. She cares deeply for others and has a rare gift for supporting them in times of deep suffering and at the end of life. She loves her family immensely. She is the best-dressed eighty-year-old Nana on the block and values good manners and kindness. Mom has been an amazing support to my dad and has always been there for her daughters. I am definitely a "mama's girl" and proud of it! If I can be like my mom in any way, I am blessed.

My dad is the most generous, hardworking man I know. The magnitude of his generosity has forever been imprinted on my life. And his work has always involved things of the heart—building and protecting Baker Roofing Company for over sixty years (which his beloved grandfather started in 1915), supporting and helping nonprofits raise money for worthy causes, learning in many years of Bible studies, and making sure our family spends time together every year on a fabulous vacation.

As a little girl, some of my fondest memories were going to my dad's office on the weekends while he worked. I played receptionist by speaking over the intercom, ate moon pies out of the vending machine, and left surprise notes on my dad's desk that he found when he got back to work Monday morning.

What I love most about my dad is the way he genuinely loves others. No matter a person's title or story, his door is open, and he is always available to listen and talk. He is never better than another. To him, every person is equal and important.

Because of my dad's intense work ethic, my mom's support at home, and God's blessings, we enjoyed a very comfortable childhood. It was not perfect, nor was it without challenges and uncertain times, but my parents provided very well for us.

In our family, Sunday mornings were for church. Every Sunday. These are some of my fondest childhood memories because we were all together and always knew the routine. I can still hear my dad's very southern, endearing voice say every Sunday as we drove to church, "I sure do have some beautiful girls."

My sisters and I were also very involved in church: youth group, acolytes, torchbearers, and Sunday school. But what we didn't do was read the Bible. I didn't read it unless I grabbed one from the back of the pew because I was bored during the service. Church was special in that it meant good friends, playtime, and service, but it wasn't what God's heart yearned for most, which was for me to grow in a relationship with Him and be changed by hearing, learning, and reading His very word. I have heard it said that the church teaches us how to behave, not how to change. That's exactly how I felt.

I would rather have had it this way than no way at all because I grew to love the idea of God by going to church. I am very thankful that my parents faithfully took us to church every Sunday. And I love God because I saw how my parents love God. They showed their love for Him through their consistent commitment to attending church with their family every Sunday and through their kindness to others.

I wrote many journals to God—lots of letters, poems, and notes. I loved the idea of Him, and I knew about Him, but I didn't *know* Him or His heart. I compare it to "loving" (fond adoration) someone I follow on social media because of their content, but I don't really know them. We all know that we only get to truly know someone when we spend time with them often.

With all that I am, I wish I had read the Bible when I was younger. If I had, I truly believe one of the darkest choices of my life may not have ever happened. I have learned that, even though the Bible may appear to be a long list of "rules," the opposite is true. It is filled with benefits for the soul. It is protection and blessing. Picture a beautiful, wide-open field with a fence that represents boundaries set in place by a Father who yearns for us not to harm ourselves and keep our souls at rest. He created us, so He *knows* exactly what we need to live in peace and safety. We just have to read it, listen to it, and obey it.

I love what John Piper, a theologian who specializes in New Testament studies, says about the Bible:

> "God wrote a book. That reality blows me away every time I stop to think about it. Pages and pages of God, His thoughts, His words, His heart. Right there, just a few inches away."[I]
>
> —John Piper

One of my favorite Bible teachers is Kristi McLelland. In her Bible study, "Gospel on the Ground," she explains, perfectly, why the Bible does what it does in us: "Keeping the Lord's laws (instructions) helps us live on God's path and attaches us to the living God. The Scriptures are like an adhesive. They bind us to the Lord in shalom and wholeness."[II]

As I grew into my teenage years, I was happy but considered myself socially awkward. As I have shared, I have always felt very "uncool," as if I didn't really fit in with the crowd. I watched a lot of General Hospital and Music Television (MTV) after school, and I hardly went to parties.

Even though I stayed home more than I was out, I was far from perfect. When I had a couple of boyfriends in high school, I made a promise to myself (and God) that I would wait until marriage to have sex. I wanted so badly to be just like my mom, who was a virgin on her wedding day. I truly thought that abstaining from intercourse itself was the most important commitment, and that it made you a virgin. But that is a lie.

I wasn't sexually pure anymore, although I thought I was without having intercourse. "Messing around" at a young age made it easier to eventually break the "big" promise about actual sex in just a few years.

Like I said, the first thought of my teenage years is always "awkward." I wasn't super social, so I'm thankful I had a small group of great girlfriends who were perfect friends for me. We still talk today, even after our lives split when we went to different colleges.

I grew up going to Wake Forest football and basketball games throughout my entire childhood because my dad was an alumnus. When my parents got married in college, they lived in married housing on the Wake Forest campus. Naturally, I went to Wake Forest University, the only college to which I applied and wanted to attend. It was the perfect place for me: small and familiar.

I would never have guessed that what I'm sharing here would be part of my college memories and forever part of my life story. Never would I have guessed that this "goody-goody," who didn't like to party in high school and wasn't "sleeping around," would end up in the situation I found myself just a few years later.

Did you know that teenagers account for 25-31% of abortions? But the majority of abortions are actually performed on women in their 20s, especially ages 20-24. The second-highest percentage of abortions performed is for women ages 25-29.

https://www.cdc.gov/mmwr/volumes/73/ss/ss7307a1
.htm

2 / a promise failed

I LOVED MY time at Wake Forest—I mean, really loved it. I wouldn't have wanted to be anywhere else. It was really special being at the same college my dad and uncle attended, plus my older sister Kim was there for three of my four years. I also met the most wonderful girlfriends at Wake Forest, who are still some of my closest friends today.

The classes were small, the campus wasn't overwhelming, the academics were top-tier, and I had a good balance between my social life and studying. And the biggest bonus was that it was only an hour and forty-five-minute drive back home to see my parents.

Before starting college, I already knew I wanted to major in psychology. Once I got into classes in my major, my favorite was Adolescent Psychology—probably because I wanted to work with teenagers since I was a teen.

My love for learning, especially this content, continued, and I did well in school by working hard. In the end, I graduated Cum Laude, received an excellent education, met some of the best girlfriends in the world, cheered Junior Varsity (JV) one year, and met my future husband. You can see why I loved it so much!

It was freshman year that this southern girl met her Jersey boy, Ricky Proehl. It was not love at first sight. In fact, it was quite the opposite. My nickname in high school was "No Joke Baker," so imagine meeting a guy who loved to pick on me and make fun of me in every little way.

Ricky was a cocky, confident, cute football player. His personality drove me mad! I couldn't stand him. He'd walk by my college dorm room on his way to his girlfriend's room and regularly throw out jokes about me. Today, he would tell you he was flirting and that was his way of showing affection. Back then, I thought he was totally obnoxious.

It wasn't until the spring semester of our freshman year that I thought he might have a nice bone in his body. (If he had the keyboard right now, I am sure he'd have plenty to say about me.) I was packing my car outside of our dorm for a road trip to Fort Lauderdale for spring break, and for whatever reason, he stopped to help. I remember thinking, *Umm, maybe he isn't a total jerk.* The thought was fleeting because I had recently broken up with my longtime boyfriend and was having fun imagining dating new guys. Ricky had also recently ended a long-term relationship and was dating other girls.

Our relationship grew from packing the car together that day freshman year to hanging out more as friends our sophomore year. Then, during the summer between sophomore and junior year, I was a camp counselor, and Ricky and I exchanged written letters back and forth. Our relationship was growing, but we weren't officially dating.

We returned to school for the fall of our junior year, and Ricky was really busy with football. He had a prolific football career, and the buzz about being drafted by the NFL grew louder. When we saw each other in the stolen moments of our busy schedules, there was a spark; it was more than friendship. We had an undeniable attraction, but our dating relationship didn't start until the spring of our junior year. We were both at a local club, Chez Andres', one night with our friends, and Ricky asked me to slow dance. That night we had our first kiss, and the rest is history.

If you know Ricky, then you know he is the life of the party. One of my favorite things about him, to this day, is how happy he is—he comes home from twelve-hour work-days laughing and smiling. He can make anything funny. He just brings great energy to most everything. And he is extremely strong mentally—there is no lack of confidence. As I began writing this book, I asked him about our relation-ship in college, and fittingly, he smirked and said, "You were obsessed with me. You were starting to realize how cute and smart I was."

He wasn't wrong. I was totally enamored. I seriously think I (the "goody-goody") was attracted to his "bad boy" side. He was tough and rugged, fun and flirty.

Ricky loved to party and had a huge personality. He came to my dorm room in the early evenings, then had to sneak out the back door and jump a wall to leave because it was so late. I would sneak into his dorm room at night when I wasn't supposed to be there, and one time, I got caught by a coach. I spent a lot of nights in his dorm room and even found myself missing more classes than I should, especially in my senior year. He was like a drug to me emotionally, physically, and mentally.

We were like most college couples: we had stupid fights, and we would break up and get back together, drink too much, and let Satan lure us into his dirty playground. That promise I made to myself not to have sex until my wedding day failed miserably. We weren't mature enough spiritually to avoid fiery lust and dark dorm rooms alone. Add in a night of drinking, and all inhibitions were out the window. I was also incredibly insecure, and once I crossed that sexual line with him, I wanted him to myself even more. I was weaving a web that would eventually get so messy that there would be no return.

Our romantic relationship deepened during our senior year. He met my family in Raleigh, and I went home with him to New Jersey to meet his family. Our parents and siblings got to know each other. We had fallen in love. We were young and growing up … and having sex.

We didn't think much past the next few months. We were playing Russian roulette, assuming nothing would happen. It was immaturity, ignorance, and defiance at its finest. Even more, I was far from understanding that sex is a spiritual connection between a man and a woman. The battle had started.

In those days, my girlfriends and I attended church on Sundays every so often—nothing consistent, but we loved the idea of God and had it in our hearts to go sometimes. But once again, I didn't have a Bible or read one. I didn't attend any small group in college or anything Bible-related. I didn't read scripture, hear scripture outside of church, or in any way know the power of God's Word to help me navigate a time of life when the enemy of our souls knows we are very vulnerable.

Throughout my journey of healing and wanting to understand the spiritual implications of sex fully, I came upon an excellent book by Paula Rinehart called *Sex and the Soul of a Woman*. Rinehart, the author of several books on relationships, is also a marriage and family counselor in Raleigh, North Carolina.

She explains a perspective on sex that I had never considered, which deeply resonated with me. In my opinion, it makes sense when I think of the Bible, and how God clearly lays the boundaries of sex within the marriage covenant to keep our souls fulfilled and safe, and that outside of marriage, sex can cause deep wounds and long-lasting shame. Rinehart says:

> As much potential as sexual intimacy has in a marriage to bless and bond a couple, it has, outside the union of a husband and wife, a commensurate ability to create havoc. It brings not life and love but bondage. The phrase often used is soul tie, meaning that married or not, starry-eyed lovers or casual acquaintances, two individuals are knit together in ways that affect them long after their sexual encounter. Something transpires between them, on a spiritual level at least, that bleeds over into other relationships and other parts of their lives...So sex is always more than just sex. You and I cannot engage in something with our bodies with-

out our hearts and souls being affected…Women, especially, spend a lot of energy trying to convince themselves that sex should not matter so much … You can't share this kind of intimacy with a man and brush it off lightly—not without becoming dead on the inside. The bonding aspect of sex is so real that outside its rightful context it becomes a form of bondage.[III]

So, maybe, with some of these insights, we can start to understand why God said sex is meant to be within the parameters of marriage. It was not to keep something pleasurable from us outside of it, but to be *for* us, to protect our hearts and souls.

There is a scripture in the Bible that says, "For this reason a man shall leave his father and his mother and be joined to his wife; and they shall become one flesh" [Genesis 2:24 New International Version (NIV)]. To that point, Rinehart noted that "the Hebrew word for joined means 'to adhere.' The glue, amazingly enough, is sex. God creates the superglue of the soul, a glue strong enough to create a bond that lasts a lifetime … If you try to pull apart two objects that have been glued together, parts of one will be stuck to the other."

I believe there is a beautiful mystery in sex that mirrors God's pursuit of you and me. He will tenderly draw us to Himself because He knows that in Him, and only Him, we are complete. Sex is a picture of His relentless, pure, and holy adoration of us. This may sound crazy if you haven't read much of the Bible or know the character of God, but consider this additional observation from Rinehart to help clarify:

> At the heart of the mystery of sex is a God who pursues you to the end of the earth, not to pin you into submission, but to embrace you at the core of your being with a love beyond that of any man, a love that penetrates to your deepest fears and heals your shame, a love that will not let you go. We are never truly free until our hearts are ravished in the love of God. This is what the mystery of sex has been trying to tell us all along.[IV]

3 / The Lie

"God doesn't stop the bad things from happening;
that's never been part of the promise. The promise is:
I am with you. I am with you until the end of time."
—*Madeleine L'Engle*

IF TWO PLUS two equals four, then unprotected sex, time and time again, will most likely lead to pregnancy. Just as Ricky and I were embarking on what should have been the thrilling adventure of our adult lives after graduating from college in May of 1990, we found ourselves pregnant.

The Phoenix Cardinals had just drafted Ricky into the National Football League (NFL), and I was headed to Atlanta, Georgia, for training as a Delta Airlines flight attendant. Being a flight attendant at that time made it easier to spend time with Ricky, who was heading west, and my family, who were east. Plus, I would get to see the world.

I was not ready to embark upon the next step in my education—graduate school for a master's in counseling. Being a flight attendant with one of my college best friends, Kathryn, was a great option at the time and allowed us to stay together for a couple more years.

It is still painful to recount these days because the raw, brutal truth is inescapable. No matter how hard I try to run from it in my mind, even today, the choice we made to abort our child is always staring at me with glaring, burning eyes.

Honestly, I don't remember much of that time, which is not unusual for those of us who are post-abortive. The mind has a clever way of blocking horrific, traumatic memories. God is gracious and protective in this.

I don't remember where I did the pregnancy test to confirm that I was pregnant. I don't remember telling Ricky. I don't even remember the clinic's exact location in Charlotte, North Carolina. I do remember bleeding some and thinking I was miscarrying, but I wasn't.

I didn't tell any of my close college friends. I only remember telling very few family members. This alone speaks of the darkness and shame I was already feeling and burying.

And what stings the most ... I had absolutely no personal inhibition. *Nothing* made me think twice. I wasn't pressured. No one told me to do it or not.

Not my brain.

Not my heart.

Not my conscience.

Not the church.

Nothing.

I don't blame anyone now, not even myself, but the truth of our abortion never goes away. To heal, I had to accept that I did the best I could with whom I was at the time. I am not saying that in any way does "whom I was" make the abortion "okay." If I were, I wouldn't have written this book. I am saying that *if* I had forever dwelt on who I was when I made the gruesome decision, then I couldn't have healed from the shame and guilt. I had to move forward.

I want to say something very, very important here. I did not understand what abortion truly was. I firmly believe I also didn't think abortion was wrong, that I was murdering our baby, or that it was a sin (rebellion and separation from a Holy God). It just wasn't discussed. It was also legal and readily available. It was an "easy solution."

On top of all that, I wasn't reading the Bible to know God's heart, so I didn't know His voice, much less hear it. Satan was doing a stellar job of keeping the reality of this heinous act silent—and keeping me blind and completely indifferent.

Years later, the tide began to turn, and a light was shed on the truth about abortion. The truth of it became much clearer and better understood. I thank God that many young girls and women began to understand that abortion kills a human life at conception, and it is far from healthcare. We may do a clever job of covering that up in our hearts, but deep in our souls, most of us know the reality of it. Abortion is Satan's dark and evil scheme, and it steals. It steals peace, rest, and joy from the soul, and it most certainly steals the chance of life for the baby.

My abortion was as casual as going out for lunch. I assumed life would go on as always. I would go onto the next step of life like it was "supposed to be." Right? New jobs, new adventures, dreams, plans...or so I thought.

It was mid-morning but sunny and hot. I felt sick to my stomach leading up to the procedure that morning; I was dreading it (like any uncomfortable gynecological procedure), not knowing how it would feel physically.

I never thought about the emotional, mental, and spiritual consequences. My body trembled inside from the unknown. I just wanted it done so I could get to Atlanta to start my job. I wanted the uncertainty of the ordeal over, the recovery done, and everything forgotten.

Ricky was already in Arizona for his new career. The waiting room was full. I was sure women were there for all types of appointments, but now I know—at the time I was there, they would have been mostly scheduled for abortion procedures. The abortion pill was not available then.

It felt like an assembly line—one woman after another. Sit and wait, get called back, have the procedure, and go home. Next woman. Next baby.

If a pregnancy test was done, I don't recall. My guess is that a test wasn't done because abortion centers are all about the money. They wouldn't want women to know if they were no longer pregnant. If an ultrasound was done, I never saw it. Now I know why—because women would see their baby and many would change their mind.

After the procedure, we went home, and I bled for days with awful cramps. It was terrible. I didn't have any physical health complications; however, many women can. Some women may never conceive again; some women may even die.

I was literally saying to myself, "Just get past this and you can forget about it and start your exciting next chapter." I felt very emotionally overwhelmed. Phone conversations with Ricky focused on moving on with our lives. Little did I know that this choice would torment me for years to come. The temporary physical pain wouldn't compare to the permanent emotional pain.

Here is the LIE: the enemy of our soul, Satan who is the father of lies, tells us, "This will all go away; you won't think of this ever again; it's an easy fix; it's not a human yet; you have too much life ahead to have a baby right now; it's not the right time; it won't be fair to the baby; you don't have enough money." And … this leads me to the real lie I told myself (and many do the same): *inconvenience.*

I see, now, that abortion is the ultimate act of selfishness. Ricky and I chose abortion, simply and brutally, because it was *inconvenient* to have a baby (and money wasn't even an excuse for us). I see it clearly now: a baby is a baby when it's convenient. At six weeks of conception, ten weeks, twelve weeks … when we plan for one, try for one, dream of one … then he or she is a baby. We celebrate. It's a baby when we miscarry and grieve, but when it's inconvenient, he or she becomes disposable and no longer valuable.

I asked Ricky to share his thoughts, to which he said:

> The couple we are now would never do that. Back then, we were young and starting our careers. You were

going to Atlanta to train with Delta, and I was going to Phoenix to start my NFL career. The timing was bad. We weren't ready to have children. We were going separate ways with our careers, and making the team for me was unknown. We knew we'd be together one day, but there were so many questions with the timing of everything. Now, we know those things aren't important. God and family are most important. If we were the people then, that we are today, we would've gotten married and had the baby.

When I hear Ricky's words today and think of my own thoughts back then, they reveal everything I need to know about our hearts, our view, our relationship, and our understanding of God. "I, me, timing, unknown, questions..." Those words say it all. Our reasons were all about us, and *nothing* about the new, precious miracle growing inside me or the heart of a Holy, loving God who creates life.

I am sure many of you reading this are thinking, "How is it possible not to know such a heinous act was wrong?" But that's the brutal truth. I spoke with my dear friend Amy (her story is in this book), who is twice abortive, and she agreed. Neither she nor I thought it was wrong. Again, it was readily available and legal. That made a huge difference for us back then. As long as abortion is legal, I can't help but think it'll always be the same for women.

It has been very hard to find the right words to write about my parents within my story, simply because I love them so very much and don't want them to feel blamed.

However, I do wish some things had been different, and they know that.

Do I wish I remembered my dad holding me and saying, "We will figure this out. Will we make it work?" Yes. Do I wish I remembered him fighting to protect me and the baby, begging me to keep the baby? Yes. Maybe Dad didn't have the chance to do these things because I honestly can't remember how much he knew.

Do I wish I remembered my mom using her nurturing gifts to promise me that I'd be okay and I could do it? Yes.

Do I wish Ricky had been stronger than me and demanded we keep our baby? Yes.

But none of these scenarios happened. These are additional gut-wrenching feelings that surround my abortion. They conjure emotions that swirl in my mind that I'd do anything to throw into a fire and burn. Either way, these conversations didn't happen, and we all must live with the outcome. That outcome has caused a lot of pain and regret for *all* of us.

When I talked to my dad about that time, he graciously said, "Any disappointment and sadness I have today is that I don't have a ninth grandchild."

The choice to have the abortion was my decision, not theirs. Ultimately, I walked into that clinic. To heal, I had to process all these ugly emotions with God and forgive any role my parents and Ricky had in my story. It was impossible to heal until I was willing to forgive them and myself—and I would have needed to do that even if they weren't sorry.

Obviously, Ricky is a big part of my story. Many may wonder why I write from my perspective alone. The answer is simple: God asked me to write this book, not him. As I've shared, Ricky has his own story. Like me, he has had to confess his sin of abortion to God and surrender to Him. But in God's beautiful way, He has also healed us together as we have sought the Lord over the years.

There have been countless moments I've felt God holding Ricky and me together. Most of these moments occur in quiet, sacred times, like in church praising God together or during long talks about our years together, the abortion, and other things. When we talk, we can see His hand on us, how He has brought us to where we are today—stronger than ever— because of a life surrendered completely to Him. We are far from perfect; whew, we fail daily, but we know who to run back to in those moments. Being held together by God in our marriage is the greatest feeling ever. It's secure and freeing.

4 / *blinded in apathy*

I WANDERED BLINDLY in my wilderness for nine years after my abortion. It was a time of intense denial and numbness. It was also an extremely busy time in my life. Over those nine years, God, in His mercy, gave us three beautiful children. We moved over twenty times during Ricky's NFL football career, and to this day, I cherish it as an incredible adventure. We lived in Phoenix, Seattle, Chicago, St. Louis, Charlotte, and Indianapolis over a span of seventeen years—all beautiful cities that gave our family unforgettable memories.

We moved every six months, keeping Greensboro, North Carolina, our "home-home" in the spring, and settling into the city where Ricky played football in the fall. Life was hectic, to say the least! It's easy to ignore painful events in our past when we keep busy. There were countless apartments, new preschools, elementary schools, sports teams, new friends, and new churches.

Having grown up in the church, it was a priority for me to take our kids to church each weekend. In every new city, I found a church for the kids and me to attend on Sunday mornings while Ricky was preparing for game day.

God was pursuing me, knowing what was coming. He knew there would never be anything or anyone else that could give my soul peace other than Him. This is His tender, relentless heart. His pursuit wasn't like a billboard or flashing lights. It was Him who gave me the simple desire and commitment to raise our children in the church and honor Him on Sunday mornings, just as my dear parents did for me. In His divine wisdom and gentleness, He knew how to woo me.

I have no doubt He is doing the same for you at this very moment. Your reading this book is His tender heart carrying you to Himself. He did not want me to remain blind and apathetic when the truth of my abortion hit me, and neither does He want that for you. He *yearns* for you to be saved, forgiven, set free, and to live in peace, freedom, and joy.

The world will tell you it can fulfill you, but we were made to know the living God and make Him known, so true fulfillment is only possible through Jesus. I see the beauty of this season of life and how each season has prepared me for where I am today. God prepared me to walk this journey just like He has prepared *you*. After all, our God is most gracious and never wastes pain if we surrender it to Him, trust Him, and let Him use it for good.

As I've shared, moving every six months was exhilarating and exhausting. I loved the adventure of new cities and new friends. I met some of the most wonderful wives in the NFL, and they are still very special friends today. I loved the game of football (and still do), and I loved watching Ricky play for seventeen years. But the stress of moving so often with three young children, a poor diet, the excitement of games, playoffs, and Super Bowls took its toll. The stress of life in general took a toll.

Eventually, my health began to decline, and I was diagnosed with an autoimmune condition called Hashimoto's Thyroiditis. It is an immune system disorder that causes a drop in hormone production from the thyroid gland, triggering a series of symptoms such as fatigue, brain fog, muscle weakness, and even depression for some people.

I believe that one of the underlying causes of my health issues that I still needed to face was the trauma of the abortion. I was in the process of getting ready to learn that until I addressed it, I could show up every day like I was okay, but deep down, I would continue to struggle. Now that I understand the various root causes of Hashimoto's, I realize that all of these stressors on my system, combined with the stress on my soul, greatly affected my overall health.

An article was published on long-term mental health in women who have had an abortion. The study found that women who had an abortion were more likely to be hospitalized for a psychiatric disorder, a substance use disorder, or a suicide attempt, within five years.

https://www.sciencedirect.com/science/article/pii /S0022395625003309?via%3Dihub

---

A helpful book to better understand how trauma, like abortion, affects our physical health is *The Body Keeps the Score* by

Bessel van der Kolk, MD. I share this because it's not only important for us to find spiritual healing after abortion, but total healing is also tied to our overall physical health, which may require healing as well.

Looking back, I realized the busyness of life was keeping me blind from seeing the truth of my abortion and facing its horrific reality. I was in church often and heard many pastors teach numerous sermons over those years. These teachings were sounder than anything I had heard before, which I believe was part of God slowly opening my heart.

But as crazy as it sounds, I still wasn't thinking about the abortion. Ricky and I didn't talk about it. Life just went on. There was no remorse or thought of the sin we had committed, but again, God was still pursuing me in His gentleness and fierce love.

If you know anything about Satan, the father of lies and deception, this is precisely his scheme—to live self-absorbed and numb our lives from confessing sin, which steals the abundant life Jesus died for us to have. Picture the movie "The Lion King" when Simba runs away to escape Scar and finds himself in the wasteland, meeting Pumbaa and Timon. Sin is the wasteland, with carcasses, rotted wood, and destruction. There is no water or spiritual life in the wasteland. True repentance is changing direction and where the living water flows—where God's forgiveness finds us. It's where He refreshes us and we are reconciled back to Him, as indicated in Acts 3:19-20 (NIV).

Repentance is a beautiful gift from God; His kindness leads us to want to repent, and in turn, He wipes away what we've done to separate ourselves from Him. There is a life-or-death difference between worldly sorrow (or remorse) that leads to spiritual death, as referenced in 2 Corinthians 7:10 (NIV), and Godly sorrow that leads to eternal life.

If you are not familiar with repentance or feel it's too "churchy," here is a simple, fantastic explanation of repentance by Dr. Rob Reimer. In his book, *The Tenderness of Jesus,* he says: "Repentance is returning to the safety of God's house. This is why God calls us to follow Him, and when we wander, He calls us to repent. He is calling us back home, into His presence. It isn't with judgment that He calls us home; it is with the tender heart of love."

As was my case, I was not yet aware that abortion was a sin. But that can change, as it did for me. I soon learned that until I confessed and repented, there would be a block in my relationship with the Lord, and it would continue contributing to my autoimmune disease. It was crucial for me to repent to receive true release from my spiritual bondage. True repentance meant I wasn't just sorry or remorseful, but I would never commit the sin again. He wanted to restore me and make me new.

So ... I had no remorse or thought of abortion as sin until ...

We were living in Seattle when Ricky played for the Seahawks. It was 1995, and I was invited to my very first small-group Bible Study. I needed to buy a Bible, but I didn't know which version to choose, so I asked the Bible study leader. She suggested the New International Version.

There was something expectant in my heart about getting my first Bible and studying with a group of ladies. But I had no idea what God was about to do in my life or how He had, thus far, orchestrated events to lead me to this very moment. This was the beginning of the Holy Spirit waking me to the light of the Truth, and Him gently revealing the darkness that had become my comfortable apathy.

"I have come into the world as a light,
so that no one who believes in me
should stay in darkness" (John 12:46 NIV).

†

During my journey, I discovered that, for me, God made certain kinds of music a *powerful* way to connect with His heart for healing. Music can connect us with his heart in a way that words can't.

At the end of each chapter, from this point on, I will share a song that I hope you will stop and listen to. Each song has played a significant role in my healing, and I pray that each one does the same for you. I hope you'll find a quiet moment to listen, not only with your ears, but also with your heart.

Song to stream:

Casting Crowns. "All Because of Mercy." Track 8, *The Very Next Thing.* SC Music, 2016, MP3.

5 / *baka*

IN PSALM 84:5-7 (NIV), "baka" means "valley of weeping or a dry season" in most translations. This Psalm describes a beautiful journey through hard seasons of life, ultimately finding refreshment in God and longing to get closer to Him:

> ⁵Blessed are those whose strength is in you,
> whose hearts are set on pilgrimage.
> ⁶As they pass through the Valley of Baka,
> they make it a place of springs;
> the autumn rains also cover it with pools.
> ⁷They go from strength to strength,
> till each appears before God in Zion.
>   (Psalm 84:5-7 NIV)

Reading my first Bible and studying it with other women was exhilarating. Spending time in God's Word did precisely what it is meant to do—personally transform me. It also put me on a pilgrimage through my own baka—a valley of weeping. God knew I needed this refining for freedom.

I was nervous and unsure about how I'd fit into the small-group Bible study. I had to be brave and ignore any hesitations, and it was worth it. Joining this group fostered a feeling of completion that I had never experienced before. My heart would pound with excitement during our studies and for hours after. I discovered how alive and active the Word of God truly is!

At first, I was mostly quiet in the group, listening and learning, but as I got more comfortable, I began to share. The beautiful thing about group studies is that everyone grows together, and no matter how long someone has been reading the Bible, we all still have a lot to learn.

I found out quickly that God is always teaching us. We never "arrive." Even to this day, I attend small-group studies with women who grew up learning Bible stories. At times, I feel "behind," but that's not how we should feel. God meets us right where we are on our unique journeys, and He uses each person to help the others grow.

As I read my first Bible, I had to seriously consider if I even had salvation in Jesus Christ. As I've shared, I grew up loving God, but I wasn't living like a follower of Jesus. I was living for my natural desires and wrapped up in my busy, self-life. Once I recognized my focus on my own desires and wants, I told Jesus that I wanted my life to be His.

I knew I needed a Savior because the Bible was lovingly teaching me that I wasn't good, nor did I seek God, even when I tried my hardest. I fell short, and I am a sinner. But I made sure I was saved.

I asked Jesus to come live in my heart and be the Lord of my life from that day forward. I asked forgiveness for all my sins and thanked Him for being my substitute on the Cross. I thanked Him for His patience with me and for His incredible kindness in drawing me to Him so I could have eternal life. At that moment, the Holy Spirit filled me and would do His job in me if I stayed close to Him. Much of what I write from here is the work of the Holy Spirit, and we will talk much more about Him in the chapters to come.

As I kept reading the Bible, scriptures came to life and pierced my heart. I started to see my abortion for what it was. I was learning the heart of God—a God of love, life, and creation.

I believe the Lord, in His Holiness and kindness, brought the abortion to the forefront of my mind, out of the buried, numb places in my heart. I learned that if I found myself mad at Him for the loss of our baby, He could handle it. (Like many people, I have a clever way of displacing blame when I don't want to be accountable.) I believe He didn't want me to live in this bondage, even though I didn't even realize how far I was from the abundant life He desired for me.

Life seemed so good. I had everything I wanted according to the world's standards, but not what I truly needed to free my soul.

This was not an easy time. It was very heavy spiritually, emotionally, and physically. Some days, it was hard even to breathe. I was fatigued, laden with guilt, filled with profound grief, anger, and broken in sorrow. My soul was shattered, and my body felt it. I was mostly alone because

Ricky was very busy with football and on his own journey with God.

It's difficult for me even to admit that, but the truth is, we all journey with God differently, and we were not ready to discuss the heinous reality of what we had done. I certainly wasn't prepared to share it with anyone else. This scripture describes exactly how I felt: "When I kept silent, my bones wasted away through my groaning all day long" (Psalm 32:3 NIV).

In a quiet, fully surrendered moment, filled with deep remorse and humility, I repented specifically of my sin of abortion to God. I believed His Word in 1 John that says, "If we confess our sins, he is faithful and just and will forgive us our sins and purify us from all unrighteousness" (1 John 1:9 NIV), and "If I had cherished sin in my heart, the Lord would not have listened" (Psalm 66:18 NIV).

I began to see light in the cracks, and I could feel His love healing my heart. I was in awe of how God had drawn me closer to Himself through a simple invitation to a Bible study. In His kindness, He knew I needed to confess my abortion as sin, and He knew I needed Him for forgiveness.

What God does this? The One True, living God—the Lord Jesus Christ! He yearned for me to know the soul-freedom He offers, and I responded in faith. I was experiencing an authentic connection with the living God and wanted to keep leaning in.

One of the many reasons I love the Psalm scripture at the beginning of this chapter is that it reminds me that those who are truly seeking God, honestly wanting to know Him, are strengthened. But we must *choose* to draw closer to God, and in getting closer, we may very well go through our own baka. But the other side is glorious. It's okay to grieve and grow simultaneously while we heal.

As the wound in my soul was slowly being healed, I continually felt God's kindness and gentleness, but I was also faced with a crushing reality ... I could hardly stand looking at myself in the mirror. I saw myself as a murderer. I believed I deserved to be in prison or on death row, for that matter.

This brutal truth became increasingly real to me as I processed what I had done. I alone had been my baby's source of life, and I had taken that away, resulting in her death. Period. I was disgusted with myself. Moreover, we had two children at this time, when the heinous truth was hitting me, and seeing what miracles they were made me hate myself even more.

It was extremely difficult not to be angry at Ricky and my parents at this time; it was easier to blame someone else than blame myself. But over time, God showed me that I could not deflect blame to heal. When I looked in the mirror, I had to remember His mercy toward me because that is Who He says He is, not believe the enemy of my soul telling me I was a murderer. I was forgiven once and for all, and I had to rely on that truth.

I could have very easily stayed in that bottomless, black abyss, but I *chose* to continue my pilgrimage, my baka, *in His light*. The enemy wanted nothing more than to sabotage my peace and keep me in a place of bondage. I chose to press on with God. It was a daily choice (still is), and although I could feel God waiting in love, He wouldn't force me to choose Him; that was up to me—daily.

I was falling more in love with the Bible. I loved doing studies with other ladies. I loved that the Bible gave me inner strength and joy.

My circle of friends began to include more women who loved Jesus. I did countless small studies with friends in the off-season and with NFL wives during the season.

Ricky was playing for the 1999 St. Louis Rams "Greatest Show on Turf" Super Bowl team, which was an epic year in the NFL, but we had our own greatest show going on in our wives' Bible study. God showed up in such significant ways as we dug into His Word together.

The Holy Spirit was clearly evident in our time together—it was tangible. He connected the wives on a deep level with Himself, making our bond with Him stronger and our bond together stronger. We prayed for each other, our children, our husbands, the team, and the staff. We laid hands on one another and earnestly sought Jesus together.

Looking back, I do not doubt that the prayers we said when we were together (and in our personal prayer time at home) strengthened and blessed our husbands and the team on the field. Matthew 6:33 (NIV) says: "But seek first his kingdom and his righteousness, and all these things will be given to you as well." We sought Him first and He added many blessings. That's how He works. I will always be thankful to Brenda Warner, Kurt Warner's wife, who led us so passionately and faithfully that season in our Bible study.

I eventually started Bible Study Fellowship (BSF) thanks to my dad's invitation. BSF is a free, international, in-depth Bible Study with layers of learning, teaching, and fellowship. Each yearly study lasts nine months and focuses on a specific book of the Bible or a group of books. Since they offer in-person and virtual classes in many countries and cities, I didn't miss a beat as we moved every six months for our football life.

I can genuinely say that God used the vehicle of BSF to change my life through its immersion in God's Word and small-group communities. I've participated in BSF for many years, and when I take a year off to do a different study with a group of friends, I always look forward to going back. In some of the years in BSF, I've even been honored to serve in leadership as a small-group leader. Isn't God amazing? He uses all of us when we have a heart willing to be His vessel.

The good news of the Bible isn't just good—it is great! In fact, it is beyond great, and no human words will ever be able to fully describe what it does in our souls. It's supernatural. Because of this, I began to realize that with repentance, I was forgiven. This prisoner was being freed from the darkness and chains, and you can be too, my friend.

Song to stream:

Crowder. "Come As You Are." Track 6, *Neon Steeple*. Capitol CMG Publishing, 2014, MP3 and CD.

6 / in the ordinary

NEVER UNDERESTIMATE HOW much the love of God can completely change your life in an ordinary moment. In fact, He does some of His most remarkable work in the ordinary, mundane moments.

Are you someone who chooses a word for the year? I'm not a "New Year resolution" girl, but I do love a word for the year—if God gives me one. I have had words like abide, bold, worship, and rest.

Towards the end of each year, I start praying, asking Him to give me a word for the next year that He wants to use in my life to grow my relationship with Him. I know what it is by knowing His voice (His Word) and what He is pressing upon my heart. Sometimes, He will confirm the word or idea by making it appear repetitively. Many times, it has been a word or concept in scripture that He will highlight to me.

There have been years that I didn't hear a word from Him. One year, my word was simply "Jesus." And there have been some years where, quite honestly, I felt like I failed miserably at focusing on my word or seeing God through it as the year passed.

Some years are better than others. These "words for the year" become my yearly theme, so to speak—abide in Him through life's ups and downs, be bolder for Him with my faith and in life's boundaries, worship Him despite what life has thrown at me, and rest in Him.

One of my favorite words was "ordinary," and its impact on my life has never left me. In fact, I've made it my "life word" if that's such a thing. Too often, we miss God working in the millions of ordinary moments in our lives, day in and day out, so I like remembering to look for Him in all the ordinary moments of my life. His Hand is woven through all of them.

There are numerous examples in the Bible of God using ordinary moments and ordinary people to accomplish His will, and here are just a couple:

While doing the very ordinary activity of "threshing," Gideon was called by God to help his people. Threshing is the process of separating grain from a plant, typically with a flail or a revolving mechanism. Imagine the monotony of doing this all day! "An angel of the Lord came and sat under an oak tree in Ophrah that belonged to Joash the Abiezrite, where his son Gideon was threshing wheat in a winepress to keep it from the Midianites" (Judges 6:11 NIV).

Peter was called an "ordinary" man in Acts. It says, "When they saw the courage of Peter and John and realized that they were unschooled, ordinary men, they were astonished and they took note that these men had been with Jesus" (Acts 4:13 NIV).

It was a very ordinary moment that God used to catapult my healing from my abortion. He uses *everything*—even martini bars! I was at a work event in Charlotte, North Carolina (the same city where I had my abortion). We were there to have fun with friends and share how Juice Plus+™, fruits and veggies in capsules had improved our health. Juice Plus+™ is juiced powders from over 30 fruits and veggies, packaged in capsules or chews.

Our family learned about Juice Plus+™ when Ricky was playing for the Carolina Panthers, and I was injured while training for the Disney Marathon. Ricky ate it for extra plant nutrition as a player (and later as a coach), and it made total sense to me to try it as well, given my injury and as a young mom raising three children who were often sick. The company's education is what actually started my journey to understanding the power of food—both good and bad—in our bodies.

A business partner of mine invited a woman named Jill to the martini bar that night, whom I had never met. Once we were introduced, we made small talk about her work and our families. I don't remember all the tiny details of our conversation. Still, she eventually shared that she was post-abortive and worked for a pregnancy care center in Charlotte, helping women navigate unplanned pregnancies.

In that very moment, it felt like a bright spotlight was shining just on me in the sea of people standing in that martini bar. My stomach sank with guilt, but I quickly felt hope because of my growing relationship with Jesus. During that conversation, my heart instantly connected with Jill's because of her willingness to share her abortion. I felt very safe with her.

Once we were alone, I shared that I had also had an abortion. At this point in my life, I had only shared about my abortion with a handful of people. She listened to me without flinching or showing disgust. She was compassionate and warm. You could feel it in her eyes. I knew I wanted to stay in touch with her, so I was bold and asked for her contact information.

All of these very ordinary moments led me down a path of deeper healing and soul-freedom. At the time, I didn't fully understand how divine and appointed that brief conversation was. For me, it started as a typical, casual night. It was a short interaction with a new friend in a loud, busy martini bar. But God's presence transcends all places and things. He was in our midst, and I would soon realize that none of this was a coincidence. I was able to help people get healthier that night, but neither Jill nor I had any idea how God would use her presence to make my soul healthier.

In the days to come, I had an uncomfortable choice to make—do I reach out to Jill, whom I barely knew, or do I shrink back from what may be pivotal in my healing? In my heart, I knew I had to be courageous and act.

This is key because God can provide an ordinary, yet divine moment like this, but we can choose not to do anything with it. I was far enough along in my healing journey to feel brave and contact Jill. If you aren't there yet, keep reading God's Word and pray often for His help. Find a circle of friends whom you trust to pray for you, even if you're not ready to tell them why. I can't emphasize enough the importance of finding a friend or two to walk your faith journey with you. We were designed for community, and the enemy likes nothing more than to isolate us from each other. Don't allow yourself to be alone.

I reached out to Jill to find out more about her and what she did at the pregnancy care center. I already admired her greatly because of her vulnerability, but I learned more amazing things about the compassionate work she did with ladies considering, or determined, to have an abortion.

Jill told me about some volunteer opportunities at the care center that sounded great to me—working in the office to help women during their appointments, being part of the prayer team, and helping the medical RV team at the abortion clinic to stop cars from going to the clinic for services.

I don't think I realized at the time, like I do now, how the Lord uses our service for others to heal us. I understand now that only He can heal us cleverly, using our pain to help others navigate the painful path we've already walked, or, even better, to encourage them to avoid it altogether. To this point, one of my favorite quotes by Christine Caine, Australian activist, evangelist, author, and public speaker, is "God uses rescued people to rescue people."[V]

To volunteer at the care center, I was required to go through an abortion recovery Bible study called "Surrendering the Secret"[VI] developed by Pat Layton (because I was post-abortive). Pat Layton is the founder and President of Life Impact Network, an international non-profit ministry based in Atlanta, Georgia. The study is an eight-session Bible study designed to help women who have experienced abortion find healing from the heartbreak and shame associated with it.

The time and day that Jill was doing the study with a group didn't work with my schedule, so she offered to do it with me one-on-one. She offered her personal time to me. This is the heart she has to love others.

I went through the study with Jill as my mentor. I was surprised by how this study purged even more emotions because it specifically dealt with the many layers of abortion.

It helped reveal that I still had a lot of anger toward Ricky and my parents. I also continued to feel a deep anger toward myself, and grief for my living children who didn't have this sibling. I discovered deep, repressed remorse for the child who didn't have a chance at life, and her possible children and family. None of this was easy work. I had to rely on God's love and forgiveness to heal fully.

Once I completed the study, I understood why the care center required post-abortive women to go through it. There was more healing to be done than I realized at the time, and they needed to make sure their post-abortive volunteers were fully healed to serve others better.

This study is also where I learned to write letters to the people in my story, sharing my honest and raw feelings—uncensored. I wrote the letters, read them aloud, processed them, and prayed over them. I gave my written words to the Lord in a heart gesture by getting on my knees and sincerely saying to Him, "I give you these feelings. I will not harbor them any longer. I believe your Word when you say to be forgiven, I must forgive also. I forgive myself and I forgive them. These emotions have been too heavy for me to carry, and now I release them to You." Then, I burned the letters. Symbolically, I was acknowledging the hurt and betrayal I caused myself and felt from others, but I was also willing to give it *all* to Jesus, whom I trusted to not only carry it but also redeem it for good.

I write about this in just a paragraph, which makes it seem deceptively simple, but it was deep soul work that took time. There were many tears, prayers, and sleepless nights. It was an emotionally heavy but also freeing process. I highly recommend doing one of these abortion recovery studies with a group or someone you trust.

"Forgiven and Set Free"[VII] is another excellent study that Jill updated and revised, along with creating a companion facilitator's guide. Today, there are more local abortion recovery groups to join, along with virtual options. I will share more about these resources at the end of the book.

After completing the "Surrendering the Secret" Bible study with Jill, I jumped into different volunteer opportunities at the care center, mainly as a sidewalk pro-life advocate near the Latrobe Abortion Clinic. (My memory tells me this was not the clinic where I had my abortion.) Our hope was to stop cars headed to the clinic, ask them to pull over, and offer the abortion-minded or abortion-determined mom the opportunity to come into the medical RV for a free ultrasound and a conversation filled with love.

I must admit, standing on that sidewalk was dreadful for me because of the atmosphere around the clinic. There are all kinds of people standing around the clinic: some quietly holding signs, others shouting into megaphones. You have pro-life and pro-choice all together. It is the most tangible feeling of life and death, good and evil, that I have ever felt.

One of the most joyous days I experienced on the sidewalk was when a vehicle with a young girl (maybe fifteen or sixteen years old) and her parents stopped to speak with us. She was headed to the clinic for an abortion, and already crying when we walked up to her car. You could immediately tell she did not want an abortion, and her parents were willing to support her either way. In a quivering voice, I shared my story and the aftermath. We talked for a while and cried for most of the conversation. That day, she chose life. Glory to God!

I often think of that child today—how old he or she is, what he or she looks like, what the grandparents love to do with their grandchild, and how grateful the mother is to have kept her baby. It is beyond humbling that God uses people of all walks of life and pasts to accomplish His will. This was yet another ordinary moment where He was working.

I know He wants to use you, too. We each have our unique journey. Getting to a place of sharing your story with others, stepping into a space where you are helping others considering abortion, or wanting to heal from one, can take time. There is nothing wrong with that. Your journey will probably look very different than mine, but He will work in your life if you invite Him in. If you genuinely want Him to help you heal, then be confident that in the countless ordinary moments that make up your days, weeks, months, and years, He is orchestrating the people and circumstances to redeem everything in your life for your freedom, joy, and His radiant glory.

Song to stream:

CeCe Winans. "Believe For It." Track 3, *Believe for It.* Essential Music Publishing under Columbia/Fair Trade Services, 2021, MP3

7 / Three days

"He sent out his word and healed them;
he rescued them from the grave."
—Psalm 107:20 NIV

WHILE JESUS' DEATH and victory over the grave took place in three days, my personal journey of God resurrecting my grief to joy, and my bondage to freedom, took years— years of wrestling with my selfishness and pride, and realizing my need for repentance and true surrender. These were years not only of getting to know Jesus as a friend and Lord, but also of learning to trust Him for forgiveness and to *rely* on the love God has for me *every single day*.

As you read this chapter, keep in mind that the crucifixion of Jesus had to occur before He could be resurrected. It is the same with our healing—repentance and humility (both are dying to self) will precede it and the victory. And it all takes time. The journey of God resurrecting your grief to joy and your bondage to freedom will come. Three days don't seem long in Jesus' story, but it can be symbolic when we think of the healing process in our story. A whole lot is happening in our souls as we admit we have sinned against a Holy God.

As you journey, don't be afraid to ask God for a fresh revelation of Himself. I still do this today, and that is okay. Only He knows what we need from Him to heal. He may do this through nature, in a conversation with someone, in a random interaction, during a sermon, in your quiet time, while you're reading scripture, while listening to a worship song, while taking a walk, etc. It may not be some grandiose moment (or it could be), but a revelation in small, ordinary moments. Our job is to be still and sensitive to His voice. God is patient, and He is faithful. He loves you more than you could *ever* fathom, and *He wants you to heal.*

I have spoken to women who had an abortion and know Jesus as their Lord and Savior; they have accepted His forgiveness, yet continue to live in guilt and bondage. They confess their sin of abortion over and over.

There can be reasons for continued bondage, some of which include (but are not limited to) a lack of unconfessed sin, giving the enemy continued access, secrets still hiding in the darkness, demons, and even curses (see Resources at the back of the book). It could be opposition from the flesh (pride is an example), or all of these. My heart hurts deeply for these women (and men) because I know they want to feel forgiven.

My encouragement is to press on and move forward. Stay in authentic community. Ask God to clear the lies and fill your mind with His Truth. Worship. Give thanks. Do not give up.

In addition, it would be wise to examine whether you have truly repented, and if so, whether you genuinely believe and rely on the love God has for you.

"¹⁵If anyone acknowledges that Jesus is the Son of God, God lives in them and they in God. ¹⁶And so we know and rely on the love God has for us" (1 John 4:15-16 NIV). Are you intentionally dwelling on and continuously dependent on the Truths in God's Word?

The Greek root meaning of "rely" in this scripture is "meno"—to remain, stay, or dwell—emphasizing a state of continuous presence or dependence. It is also written as "abide" in some Bible translations. It is meant to make you aware of the choice to stay in his constant presence. Do you consciously choose to stay in his continuous presence? (Tip: Put sticky notes with scripture all over your house and in your car.) Are you living life with other Believers? Are you asking for prayer? There is an intimacy with God that is only developed over time through abiding in Him day in and day out and being in authentic Christian community.

During my early years of seeking God with my whole heart, abiding in Jesus was crucial. And it always will be. Abiding is vital for Believers. We must stay connected to the Vine, who is Jesus, as stated in John. It says, "⁵I am the vine; you are the branches. If you remain in me and I in you, you will bear much fruit; apart from me you can do nothing. ⁶If you do not remain in me, you are like a branch that is thrown away and withers; such branches are picked up, thrown into the fire and burned" (John 15:5-6 NIV).

For me, abiding looks like not getting out of bed until I've talked to Him. I thank Him, I repent of my sins, and I pray for others and my needs. Then, I keep talking to Him all day long and remind myself that I can't do anything for Him without Him, so I need to stay dependent on Him. (The vine is the source of life.) It means dropping to my knees in prayer during the day. Abiding is worshipping Him throughout the day, giving Him thanks. It's confessing sin. It's remembering that "His grace is sufficient, and His power is made perfect in my weakness" (2 Corinthians 12:10 NIV).

I also always try to remember the scriptures saying that He will prune any branch that is not producing fruit so that it will produce more fruit. This helps me when hard things happen in life that I don't understand. Abiding is the lifeline between Him and Believers during waiting seasons, mountaintops, and valleys.

We abide, we worship, we confess, we believe, we praise, we fellowship, we persevere, and we pray. We read the Bible. These are the ways we live from victory in Jesus, not for victory. If we are Believers, the battle is won. We don't have to struggle or fight for peace. We need to believe what He did for us on the Cross was sufficient—and live in that victory. Jesus conquered the grave, and His greatest desire is for you to rise again and live victoriously over your shame and guilt because His sacrifice on the Cross covered them. I love what Pastor Derwin Gray says, "Instead of reliving the trauma, relive the triumph."

I can't say enough about the importance of daily choices. As we journey to our resurrection from the grave, every single day moves us from:

curses to blessings,
darkness to light,
brokenness to healing,
despair to joy,
bondage to freedom.

The key is to move *forward*.

I have just shared a lot of general disciplines as Christians that help us live the abundant life Jesus desires for us. I'd also like to share and reiterate the specific, personal choices that I made years ago in the in-between, in the hope that these help you more specifically. Consider all the senses as you read on—what we allow our eyes to see, our ears to hear, our lips to taste, our nose to smell, and our hands to touch.

Read the Bible Daily

I chose—and still choose—to read or listen to the Bible daily (usually first thing in the morning). I much prefer reading over listening when possible. This is the key to renewing my mind daily. Hearing and reading scripture are centering, calming, comforting, and corrective, and they strengthen my connection to the living God. As I interact with scripture, His Spirit speaks to me in a supernatural way that can't be explained in human words. (I will share more about this.) I like this passage, "For the word of God is alive and active. Sharper than any double-edged sword, it penetrates even to dividing soul and spirit, joints and marrow; it judges the thoughts and attitudes of the heart" (Hebrews 4:12 NIV) as well as this one, "Do not conform to the pattern of this world, but be transformed by the renewing of your mind. Then you will be able to test and approve what God's will is—his good, pleasing and perfect will" (Romans 12:2 NIV).

In His Word, I am reminded daily of who He is, who I am in Him, and that He can do what He says He can do. I learn how to be His follower and how to live a life of abundance and peace. *Nothing* replaces reading the Bible—Jesus Himself—(not even a devotional), and in the world that we live today, we can't afford not to read it daily.

Worship, Thanksgiving, and Prayer

Worship and thanksgiving have become two of the most beautiful gifts to my soul. (This makes sense because we are all created by Him and for Him.) Both have been extremely healing. They are also weapons against the enemy of our souls.

I love to raise my hands high in a good worship song and sing of God's Glory and goodness. Tears stream down my face, whether I'm in church, in my home alone, in my car, or on a walk. Jesus shifts the atmosphere, and it's tangible!

I love to spend my prayer time giving thanks for every little and big thing in my life. I pray all day long—in my bed, on my bike, on a walk, in my car, sitting at my desk, with my friends, on the phone … the list goes on. I learned that asking others to pray for me is not a sign of weakness; it's actually a sign of great humility, and it's very powerful for others to petition God on my behalf. These habits alone will set your heart on fire and break chains. God loves gratitude, and He's not looking for eloquent prayers. He wants you to talk to Him.

I can't stress enough the power of worship and thanksgiving, and worship music, too. (That is why I wanted to include music as part of my book.) In Ann Voskamp's book *One Thousand Gifts,*[VIII] she points out that before any miracle Jesus performed, He always gave thanks. We should model Him and watch Him start performing miracles in our lives! As it says in 1 Thessalonians, "Give thanks in all circumstances: for this is God's will for you in Christ Jesus" (Thessalonians 5:18 NIV).

Repent Daily

I have also learned the obedience of repenting daily—and the freedom. I understand that confessing my sin to God daily removes anything that stands between us, and that we are commanded to do so. It's actually a very tender request from God, because He knows that when we repent, we find a refreshing mercy and a deeper intimacy with Him. Walls are broken down for more freedom, we bear more fruit, we are kinder to others, we see our shortcomings, and we acknowledge Him as Holy.

God's kindness is intended to lead us to repentance. Romans reminds us of this, "Or do you show contempt for the riches of his kindness, forbearance and patience, not realizing that God's kindness is intended to lead you to repentance?" (Romans 2:4 NIV). He can't heal what we don't admit. "In repentance and rest is your salvation, in quietness and trust is your strength..." (Isaiah 30:15 NIV).

Find a Church Home and Community

Finding true community was another crucial part of my healing. We were created in the image of a Triune God (three-in-one)—God the Father, God the Son, and God the Holy Spirit. He designed us for an authentic community for the health of our souls and also for healing. Since we were created in *His image*, He designed us for a relationship with Him and others. I am talking about open, honest, nonjudgmental friends ... a group of Jesus-loving people who don't gasp at our sins, but gasp at the awe of God over our sin. Jesus doesn't condemn His followers, so we shouldn't either. Pride and our fundamental sin-nature will keep us from opening to these friends, so we must resist that. "God opposes the proud but shows favor to the humble" (James 4:6 NIV).

I have found these friends in school, at church, in Bible studies, at work, at the gym, and by asking God to bring them into my life. It's pretty cool how He has a clever way of orchestrating friendships with people we didn't even know. I cannot imagine my life without my Jesus sisters. I don't just say that. They are treasures, and life is much, much easier with them. We celebrate the good, we walk through the bad together, we pray for one another in it all, and we are real with each other. The even bigger breakthrough comes when we move from the pride and shame of keeping secrets to humility and responsibility by sharing with others.

When you spend time with someone you love, how do you feel? I feel fulfilled and a deep joy. It's not a feeling that can be explained in words. The connection with true friends fills our souls. I believe this is partly why He uses community to help heal our brokenness. And we must be wise in choosing our friendships; their counsel and guidance can point us to Christ—or not.

I am also talking about a church home—a church that teaches the Bible and doesn't shy away from sensitive issues— not a distorted Truth or Gospel. You will have wisdom in this area as you learn God's Word, but be prayerful today because there are many false teachers out there.

> [1]Dear friends, do not believe every spirit, but test the spirits to see whether they are from God, because many false prophets have gone out into the world.[2] This is how you can recognize the Spirit of God: Every spirit that acknowledges that Jesus Christ has come in the flesh is from God,[3] but every spirit that does not acknowledge Jesus is not from God. (1 John 4:1-3 NIV)

Many churches offer Bible studies, which is a great way to connect with a small group. It has become easy today to stay home and watch church online. I admit that Ricky and I do this still in certain situations. But the church body is Biblical and essential to Jesus. This is His family, and He desires us to have a church home and be active there.

In addition, true community is vital for breakthrough. There is an important Biblical healing aspect of community, which is confessing our sins to one another:

"Therefore confess your sins to one another and pray for one another so that you may be healed" (James 5:16 NIV).

It is sobering to consider what the Bible describes as the extreme contrary when we keep our sins a secret, even from what we can rationalize to be a secret from God: "When I kept silent, my body wasted away through my groaning all day long. For day and night your hand was heavy on me; my strength was sapped as in the heat of summer" (Psalm 32:3-4 NIV).

Once we lay them down at the Cross, the forgiveness and freedom are waiting: "Then I acknowledged my sin to you and did not cover up my iniquity. I said, 'I will confess my transgressions to the Lord.' And You forgave the guilt of my sin" (Psalm 32:3-5 NIV).

Forgive Myself and Forgive Others

I touched on this in the prior chapter—another necessary choice in my healing journey has been forgiving others in my story and choosing to stop being angry with them or blaming them. Anger and blame are tools of the enemy, and in them, bitterness grows. Forgiveness demonstrates obedience to God and not to the person who sinned against us—"²¹Then Peter came to Jesus and asked, 'Lord, how many times shall I forgive my brother or sister who sins against me? Up to seven times?' ²²Jesus answered, 'I tell you, not seven times, but seventy-seven times' " (Matthew 18:21-22 NIV). Forgiveness is crucial for living in freedom and joy. It's not a feeling; it's an act of our will, a choice, and the heart catches up in time.

Unforgiveness is also a prison for your soul. God even goes so far as to say that when we don't forgive others, He won't forgive us. We must also forgive ourselves, because God forgives us when we genuinely repent. This quote from C.S. Lewis says it perfectly: "If God forgives us, we must forgive ourselves. Otherwise, it's like setting up ourselves as a higher tribunal than him."[IX] Again, this is an act of our will and a choice we make based on our belief that Jesus paid the price for our sin. It's a fact, not a feeling.

Forgiving myself and others didn't happen overnight; it came with digging in and getting to know God's heart better. As I've shared, writing letters to these people was very healing for me. I also had conversations with them, but sometimes that isn't possible. It helped me a lot to see the people in my story, much like me, as sinners. Not one of us is perfect. I messed up; they messed up. In all truth, we are all messed up.

I do understand that some women's stories are very different from mine. I may appear flippant to you if you were pressured into your abortion, raped, or experienced some other profound betrayal. I imagine forgiveness could feel insurmountable when coping with one trauma compounded by another. However, genuine forgiveness is a crucial step to healing. "[31]Get rid of all bitterness, rage and anger, brawling and slander, along with every form of malice. [32]Be kind and compassionate to one another, forgiving each other, just as in Christ God forgave you" (Ephesians 4:31-32 NIV). I truly want you to heal both physically and emotionally, and forgiveness is a significant part of the healing process. I say this only because Jesus says it.

Just as Jesus has forgiven us, we must forgive others. Give yourself grace and time. It'll feel like a layered process. You aren't saying what they did was okay; you are releasing yourself from the grip of bondage and obeying God. A hard thing to hear, but important, is that many times when we can't forgive others, it's because we don't fully understand how much grace *we* have been given. This was a red flag to me personally on my journey (and it still is today when it comes up in different life situations). This conviction should prompt us to dig in, grow in deeper intimacy with Jesus, believe in God's redemptive power to bring good to any situation, and even pray that God will bless those who curse us as written in Luke 6:28 (NIV), "bless those who curse you, pray for those who mistreat you."

These steps of forgiveness are not only necessary for healing but also pivotal for our physical health. I love what Pastor Greg Laurie says about forgiveness: "Not only is forgiveness important to you spiritually, but it is also good for your health."[X]

Several years ago, *Time* magazine published an article titled, "Should All Be Forgiven?" The article stated that "scientists and sociologists have begun to extract forgiveness and the act of forgiving from the confines of the confessional, transforming it into the subject of quantifiable research." The writer went on to say:

A number of psychotherapists are testifying that there is nothing like [forgiveness] for dissipating anger, mending marriages, and banishing depression. The world is finally coming around to see the value of what God has been saying all along. It is good to forgive. It is good for you physically. It is necessary for you spiritually. If you are truly a child of God, it is not an option. You must forgive (www.thinke.org).[XI]

There are resources at the back of this book that may help you in this area. Remember, unforgiveness and things we keep secret will also affect our physical health. I highly suggest that if you are struggling with forgiving others, bitterness, and anger over your abortion, seek a solid Christian counselor.

Personify Our Baby

Another important choice in my healing journey has been to personify our baby. It is good to say their gender and give them a name as we grieve and remember them. I feel our baby was a girl, and I refer to her as "Sweet Angel." That is what I heard from God after praying.

If you've never thought of doing this, consider it and ask God to reveal to you these details. It can be helpful to grieve him or her as a person.

Live a Healthy Life

What we eat and drink affects how we think, feel, and act. I have learned this the hard, long way. For me, this includes eating nourishing foods (real food and not a lot of processed foods or sugar), drinking lots of clean, filtered water, exercising, getting sunshine, having less stress, doing hobbies I enjoy, spending time with people I love, and maintaining boundaries from those who are toxic. I am also careful about what my eyes see and what my ears hear.

Share My Story and Serve Others

Obviously, you are reading this book, so you know I am bold enough to share my story now, which has been another powerful step in my healing, but that takes time. As you heal, pray for the courage to share your story with others, and watch how the Lord heals you even more deeply as you begin to serve others through it.

Sharing my story has involved one-on-one conversations with people. Or it's been a moment with a group of friends when I least expected to share (my heart frantically beating), then hearing them disclose that they had an abortion, too, and never told anyone. It has been sharing that I am writing this book and hearing countless women share that they had an abortion, or multiple abortions, and again, never told anyone.

Serving others through my story has looked like sitting with a friend and just listening. It has been praying for friends who are hurting and struggling with the shame and guilt of an abortion. It has meant standing on the sidewalk of an abortion clinic, praying and being available to love women headed inside for an abortion. It is being there for women after they have chosen abortion. It's been serving on the Board of a pro-life organization.

God wants us to use our pain to help others, which in turn helps heal us. God is great!

Trust God and Surrender Daily

Our walk with Christ is a daily choice. There is a war between our flesh wanting to do what it wants versus the Holy Spirit in us. I consciously choose to listen and obey the Spirit's lead. I can hear Him when I choose to be close to Him in His Word, worship, thanksgiving, prayer, and repentance. I fall short often, but I don't condemn myself. I know Jesus is waiting to pick me up again and again. I choose to live in His grace daily.

I also prefer to let Him use my story not only to bring beauty from the ashes in my life, but also to help others. I continue to trust that He will use my story for my good and the good of others.

Life is going to keep happening. We will have good days and bad. We must remember our feelings are fickle and do not determine our forgiveness or freedom. We operate on the facts of the Bible scripture. It may take time—probably longer than three days on your journey—but you are forgiven instantly when you have given your heart to Jesus and genuinely repent. Hope will rise. Joy will increase as you spend time in His Word, worshipping Him, and giving thanks, and as you spend time in fellowship with other believers. Allow the gentle embrace of our Savior to hold you. Noah walked faithfully with God as noted in Genesis 6:9 (NIV). God wants you to walk faithfully with Him, holding your hand and carrying you if you need it. This is not religion; this is a relationship with the living God.

One of the toughest days in my story came years later in my life when we were faced with telling our living children about the abortion. This was probably one of the hardest things I've done, and I'm so thankful Ricky was willing to support me in this because I had no idea how much healing it would bring to our family. It also turned out to be a tremendous gift to me—showing me that the Lord had healed Ricky, too.

I was asked to share my abortion story on a local Charlotte television show by a sweet friend and fellow football wife, Michaela Scurlock. If I were going to make a public statement for all to hear, I wanted our children to hear it from us first. I knew it was time to tell our living children. God uses friends like Michaela to bring about our healing. She has been an enormous source of encouragement for sharing my story more publicly.

I also knew I was ready to share publicly because I saw that my vulnerability was helping other women start their own path of healing with God. So, I agreed to the show, but first we wanted our children's permission to make our story public. This choice took a lot of prayer and courage because we didn't know how the kids would react and feel about us.

Coordinating schedules took a lot of effort and planning, but we were determined. Two of the kids were in college; one still lived at home. We set a time to meet at Ricky's office at our business in Greensboro, North Carolina. It would've been much easier to tell Michaela "no" and forget about it, but Ricky and I sensed how important this was to our family and others who might be struggling with the guilt of abortion.

I was much more nervous than Ricky (as usual) that day. I was dreading it, yet knew it was necessary for me to share, and not just because of the TV show. I felt that I was hiding a secret from them, and they deserved to know. I was also starting to understand the serious spiritual consequences of keeping secrets from our children.

The kids listened as we told our story. They were shocked, but they weren't angry or mad. They were calm and asked a lot of questions. It proved to be an incredibly healing moment. When I look back on that moment, I am even more thankful for their personal relationships with the Lord because they extended the same grace to us that God has given them. As abortion does, it affects many more people than just the post-abortive parents. We took a sister from our children, cousins, nieces, and nephews—a whole line of offspring.

As our three children get older, I feel like the hole in my soul gets deeper in some ways. I don't mean that my guilt and shame have come back, but I see how special our children are and how God is using them, and I feel the consequences of our decision. They each have such beautiful gifts and bring their unique talents and energy to the world. Our daughter and her husband have twin girls, our first grandchildren, which is such an incredible blessing from the Lord, but also a painful reminder of our choice as we watch them grow up.

As we come to know our Creator and His heart for life, we cherish the fact that each life created by Him is incredibly valuable, filled with poignant purpose. Each life is made in His image. But we reap what we sow, and consequences remain after our choices, even when we live in forgiveness. (They are a package deal.) As I've said, I don't live in guilt or shame now, but I know I will always have that hole in my soul filled with sadness.

Finally, to draw a full circle here, reading scripture out loud is more powerful than reading it silently. I want to encourage you to end this chapter by taking quiet time to read Psalm 103 (NIV) out loud, saying "my and me" instead of "you and yours," and feel the power of the Word:

Psalm 103 (NIV)

Praise the LORD, my soul;
all my inmost being, praise his holy name.

Praise the Lord, my soul,
and forget not all of his benefits—

who forgives all your sins and
heals all your diseases,

who redeems your life from the pit,
and crowns you with love and compassion,
who satisfies your desires with good things
so that your youth is renewed like the eagle's.

The LORD works righteousness
and justice for all the oppressed.

He made known his ways to Moses,
his deeds to the peoples of Israel:

The Lord is compassionate and gracious,
slow to anger, abounding in love.

He will not always accuse,
nor will he harbor his anger forever;

He does not treat us as our sins deserve
or repay us according to our iniquities.

For as high as the heavens are above the earth,
so great is his love for those who fear him;

as far as the east is from the west,
so far has he removed our transgressions from us.

As a father has compassion on his children,
so the LORD has compassion on those who fear him.

Amen! I hope you felt those words deep in your soul.

Song to stream:

Bethel Music and Brandon Lake. "Come Out of that Grave (Resurrection Power)." Track 16, *Revival's in the Air (Live)*. Bethel Music and Capitol CMG Publishing, 2020, Digital download (including M4A).

impactful scriptures

ON THE FOLLOWING pages, I have written scriptures that were most impactful to me as I first started reading the Bible and was waking up to the truth of my abortion. They helped me get to know God's heart. They led me to repentance, helped me to accept His forgiveness, and ushered me into the crucial habit of renewing my mind daily. We will talk about salvation in Him shortly if you are not saved and ready to give your life to Him.

"The Son of Man came to seek and save the lost" (Luke 19:10 NIV).

"Then Jesus came to them and said, 'All authority in heaven and on earth has been given to me' " (Matthew 28:18 NIV).

"I want you to know that the Son of Man has authority on earth to forgive sins" (Matthew 9:6 NIV).

"For the word of God is alive and active. Sharper than any double-edged sword, it penetrates even to dividing soul and spirit, joints and marrow; it judges the thoughts and attitudes of the heart" (Hebrews 4:12 NIV).

"Before I formed you in the womb I knew you, before you were born I set you apart; I appointed you as a prophet to the nations" (Jeremiah 1:5 NIV).

[13]For you created my inmost being;
you knit me together in my mother's womb.
[14]I praise you because I am fearfully and wonderfully made;
your works are wonderful, I know that full well.
[15]My frame was not hidden from you
when I was made in the secret place,
when I was woven together in the depths of the earth.
[16]Your eyes saw my unformed body;
all the days ordained for me were
written in your book
before one of them came to be." (Psalm 139: 13-16 NIV)

"Repent, then, and turn to God, so that your sins may be wiped out, that times of refreshing may come from the Lord" (Acts 3:19 NIV).

"Or do you show contempt for the riches of his kindness, forbearance and patience, not realizing that God's kindness is intended to lead you to repentance?" (Romans 2:4 NIV).

"This is what the LORD says—your Redeemer, who formed you in the womb: I am the LORD, the Maker of all things, who stretches out the heavens, who spreads out the earth by myself" (Isaiah 44:24 NIV).

"Against you, you only, have I sinned and done what is evil in your sight; so you are right in your verdict and justified when you judge" (Psalm 51:4 NIV).

"If we confess our sins, he is faithful and just and will forgive us our sins and purify us from all unrighteousness" (1 John 1:9 NIV).

"I, even I, am he who blots out your transgressions, for my own sake, and remembers your sins no more" (Isaiah 43:25 NIV).

[10]"he does not treat us as our sins deserve
or repay us according to our iniquities.
[11]For as high as the heavens are above the earth,
so great is his love for those who fear him;
[12]as far as the east is from the west,
so far has he removed our
transgressions from us." (Psalm 103:10-12 NIV)

"For I will forgive their wickedness and will remember their sins no more" (Hebrews 8:12 NIV).

"He brought them out of darkness, the utter darkness, and broke away their chains" (Psalm 107:14 NIV).

"Do not be anxious about anything, but in every situation, by prayer and petition, with thanksgiving, present your requests to God" (Philippians 4:6 NIV).

"Then Peter began to speak: 'I now realize how true it is that God does not show favoritism' " (Acts 10:34 NIV).

"Therefore, if anyone is in Christ, the new creation has come: The old has gone, the new is here!" (2 Corinthians 5:17 NIV).

"Therefore, there is now no condemnation for those who are in Christ Jesus" (Romans 8:1 NIV).

"God made him who had no sin to be sin for us, so that in him we might become the righteousness of God" (2 Corinthians 5:21 NIV).

"In fact, the law requires that nearly everything be cleansed with blood, and without the shedding of blood there is no forgiveness" (Hebrews 9:22 NIV).

[18]"Forget the former things;
do not dwell on the past.
[19]See, I am doing a new thing!
Now it springs up; do you not perceive it?
I am making a way in the wilderness
and streams in the wasteland." (Isaiah 43:18-19 NIV)

"The thief comes only to steal and kill and destroy; I have come that they may have life, and have it to the full" (John 10:10 NIV).

8 / the invitation

WHEN RICKY AND I were forty-five years old, we found out we were pregnant—again. Say what! Our kids were nineteen, seventeen, and fourteen. We were looking at completely starting over. We were shocked. It took a few weeks to process the news, but once we did, we were elated.

I remember feeling that this was our redemption child, that the Lord was saying, "I forgive you both; this child is a surprise like the first, but this one you will choose and love." We were willing and ready.

Every time I went to the doctor, early in the pregnancy, he emphasized the weak heartbeat of the baby. I didn't focus on that; instead, I focused on the gift of this new life.

I was very nauseous with morning sickness, which wasn't unusual for me early in my pregnancies. An ultrasound was coming up, and our middle child wanted to come with me, which I loved. Ricky was coaching for the Carolina Panthers, so he didn't have much free time, and we assumed the ultrasound was routine.

With my eighteen-year-old son, Austin, by my side, we watched the ultrasound and found that we had lost the baby.

There was no heartbeat. It made sense because my nausea had suddenly, abruptly stopped. The whole family was devastated.

A dilation and curettage (DNC) was scheduled, a minor surgical procedure performed in the uterus, and a standard treatment following a miscarriage. Thankfully, Ricky could come with me.

Before the procedure, we asked for one more ultrasound to confirm the loss of the baby. Her beautiful name was Brooklyn Rose Proehl. Again, I don't know for sure that I was pregnant with a girl, but my heart tells me that this baby was a girl, too. Giving her a name and a gender made her a person we could grieve as a family.

I still don't fully understand all the Lord had for us at that time. As it says in Isaiah, "As the heavens are higher than the earth, so are my ways higher than your ways and my thoughts than your thoughts" (Isaiah 55:9 NIV).

What I do know is that she was a gift from Him. He may have been refining us, pruning us, and maybe, just maybe, part of this experience was meant to test how we'd respond this time. I've learned in many life situations that, as I walk with God, I just have to be okay with not knowing why and trust that He is Sovereign.

When I was waking up from the DNC anesthesia, I had a very sacred, holy moment with God. I will never forget this moment as long as I am on this side of heaven. I felt as if I had been invited into His presence with the warmest, most peaceful feeling I've ever experienced. It was just me and Jesus, having a moment together. It was the best invitation

I've ever received. All I know is that I knew, really knew in that moment, the depth of His great love for me. And He loves you just the same.

Doesn't everyone love an invitation—an invitation to a wedding, a party, a lunch date, a walk, a weekend away with friends? We feel special, seen, included, like we belong. Now, I believe the greatest invitation of your life is awaiting your response if you haven't accepted it yet—giving your life to Jesus, accepting Him as *your* Lord and Savior. Or maybe you need to recommit your life to Christ—that is your invitation. It's the beginning of life—abundant life—filled with forgiveness, peace, freedom, and joy.

God saw the condition of my heart, and He sees yours, too. Don't be afraid of that. He wants nothing more than for you to know how very much He *loves* you and wants to help you find peace with Him. The door is open, but you must walk through. Even if you are mad at God for your loss, He can handle that, too. He can handle all your feelings.

Let me emphasize that Jesus is the only way to be forgiven. His blood shed on the cross is the only way we can be forgiven for the blood we shed and for all sins. This is noted in Hebrews, "...without the shedding of blood there is no forgiveness" (Hebrews 9:22 NIV).

Sin is not a popular word today, but it is imperative that we accept that sin is what God sees. It is necessary for us to see it like He does in order to heal. Sin is everything we've done or will do that separates us from a Holy God. We are *all* sinners. He tells us this in Romans, "... for all have sinned and fall short of the glory of God" (Romans 3:23 NIV).

The Bible tells us that without Jesus as our Lord and Savior, we are dead in our sins, but with Jesus, we are saved from eternal death by His blood. The blood of Jesus reconciles us back to the Father. And, the Bible says that not one of us is without sin, abortion or not. Jesus was our substitute. It should've been us on that cross, but God loves you and me so much that He sent His Son, Jesus, to die for us. And then He was resurrected and is alive! And even more, He died so we could have *abundant* life here on earth—peace and rest for our souls—beyond any ordinary, earthly feeling.

You won't find another "god" that left His heavenly realm to come to us, walked among us, suffered greatly for all our sins, and then offered us the gift of eternal life. Eternal life is life without end. When we take our last breath on earth, Believers will immediately be in the presence of Almighty God. There will be no end with Him or praising Him with other Believers in heaven.

If you haven't already, are you ready to give your life to this amazing God and be forgiven for your abortion and all your sins? If you are, here is a prayer that I wrote to say (I recommend saying it aloud), *believe,* and share with someone that you've made the most important decision of your life:

Lord, I am a sinner—not just my sin of abortion, but I was born a sinner, separated from You. I can't save myself, and I know I need a Savior to forgive me for my sins, including my abortion. Please forgive me and give me new life by Your sacrifice. I believe Your Son Jesus Christ is Your only begotten Son, was crucified on that cross in Calvary, was buried, and three days later, rose from the grave to give me NEW LIFE. I believe what I am saying, and I want to live my life in peace with You, with forgiveness, joy, and freedom. I want the abundant life in You that You promise. I surrender my life to you now, Jesus. Be LORD of my life. AMEN.

If you prayed this sincerely, I want you to tell someone. My heart sings with yours, but more than that, the God of all creation, Jesus, and the Holy Spirit are rejoicing!

The Bible says, "If you declare with your mouth, 'Jesus is Lord,' and believe in your heart that God raised him from the dead, you will be saved" (Romans 10:9 NIV). Note two essential parts to this scripture: first, confess with your mouth, *and* second, believe in your heart.

If you are struggling to believe, I encourage you to open your mind to receiving Truth and revelation from God. God is okay with your unbelief and wants you to share it honestly with Him. There is a real battle between good and evil around us. Remember, the devil is the father of lies and deception, and he doesn't want you to be freed.

Here are some suggested resources to watch, listen to, or read if you are skeptical:

- The Bible will always be the best book for revelation. I recommend starting with the book of John in the New Testament.

- Another great book to read (or movie to watch) is *The Case for Christ* by Lee Strobel.[XII] A former atheist, Strobel digs into the historical evidence for Jesus Christ, interviewing scholars to examine the New Testament and Jesus's life, ultimately leading him to embrace faith.
- Strobel also authored *Is God Real?*[XIII] An excellent book for those learning about God.
- An additional resource is C.S. Lewis, a former atheist who, after much debate with his friend J.R.R. Tolkien, came to the realization that Jesus is the Son of God. He shares the story of his transition in his autobiography *Surprised by Joy.*[XIV]
- Finally, *Evidence that Demands a Verdict*[XV] by Josh McDowell and Sean McDowell, PhD, is a compelling read to support the existence of God.

Except for the Bible, the resources listed above are examples of men who initially set out to prove that God isn't real and that Jesus isn't who He claimed to be. Through research, they changed their minds and provided proof for others to learn as well.

Simply say to God, "If you are real, show me." The Bible says, "If you seek Me with your whole heart, you will find Me" (Jeremiah 29:13 NIV). Give Him a chance.

You may have grown up in a super "religious" home where you were told God could never forgive abortion, or had someone tell you that along the way. Maybe you grew up in a home where abortion wasn't a big deal. What people say isn't the plumb line; it's what God says that matters.

So, let's consider what God says. Below are some additional scriptures that state the ultimate truth, and hopefully, will encourage you to focus on God's standard, not others' opinions, or what you've conjured in your mind. I also pray that they comfort you. (As I suggested in chapter seven, you may even want to pick your favorites, write them on sticky notes, and put them around your house and in your car):

> [4]Against you, you only, have I sinned
> and done what is evil in your sight;...
> [7]Cleanse me with hyssop, and I will be clean;
> wash me, and I will be whiter than snow.
> [8]Let me hear joy and gladness;
> let the bones you have crushed rejoice.
> [9]Hide your face from my sins and blot out all my iniquity.
> [10]Create in me a pure heart, O God, and renew a steadfast spirit within me." (Psalm 51:4, 7-10 NIV)

> "He did not discriminate between us and them, for he purified their hearts by faith" (Acts 15:9 NIV).

> "Godly sorrow brings repentance that leads to salvation and leaves no regret, but worldly sorrow brings death" (2 Corinthians 7:10 NIV).

> "Whoever conceals their sins does not prosper, but the one who confesses and renounces them finds mercy" (Proverbs 28:13 NIV).

"But you, Lord, are a compassionate and gracious God, slow to anger, abounding in love and faithfulness" (Psalm 86:15 NIV).

"...but those who seek the LORD lack no good thing" (Psalm 34:10 NIV).

From here, we can't sit idle. We must work out our salvation. This does not mean we are saved by anything *we* do— ever. It means we understand Jesus did it *all*, and we must obey and abide in Him, His Word, spend time with other Believers and our church body, and pray. By faith, we believe in what we cannot see. It's like going to the gym. We can't expect to feel better and be healthier if we go to the gym and sit on our phone the whole time we are there. This is a relationship that takes two, and He has given us everything we need to live a vibrant, abundant life with Him. We have to work it out by abiding in Him, as I shared in chapter seven, and bear fruit for Him.

I also highly encourage you to get baptized. Baptism is a public proclamation of what you've declared (faith, repentance, and new life). I was "christened" as an infant in the Episcopal church, but that is not the baptism that Jesus speaks of. In Matthew, it says: [19]"Therefore go and make disciples of all nations, baptizing them in the name of the Father and of the Son and of the Holy Spirit, [20]and teaching them to obey everything I have commanded you. And surely I am with you always, to the very end of the age" (Matthew 28:19-20 NIV).

It is an outward expression and affirmation of faith that we make of our *own* accord, not at the decision of our parents or others. I was baptized at the age of forty-seven. It's never too late, but I wish I had done it earlier, when I really started following Jesus in my thirties, to declare Jesus was my Lord and Savior publicly.

Part of not sitting idle is also to be aware that the enemy of God—Satan—will try his best to make you doubt your salvation and forgiveness. We have to stand on Truth (not feelings) and stay close to those walking out their faith, too. Remember, God designed us to be in community. Satan wants nothing more than for us to isolate and be alone. I can't emphasize this enough. The enemy wants us to live in our own private religion, in shame, so we don't find freedom and joy through true community and confession. You have a choice to live in freedom with Christ or bondage with Satan.

Through Jesus, we have not only been saved from the wrath of our sins and hell, but it gets even better! When we accept Jesus as Lord and Savior of our lives, He comes to live inside us as the Holy Spirit. (God three-in-one: the Father, the Son, and the Holy Spirit). Jesus explained that it was better for him to leave because then the Holy Spirit would come live inside us and be with us wherever we are.

I often think how kind the Father is to give us this incredible gift! The Holy Spirit is the Spirit of Truth. He is our counselor, teacher, comforter, and guide. Oftentimes, we hear He is a dove or the wind, but He is a person—Jesus Christ living in us. What an incredible gift! The world (non-Believers) cannot see Him because they neither see Him nor know Him, as noted in John, "The Spirit of truth. The world cannot accept him, because it neither sees him nor knows him. But you know him, for he lives with you and will be in you" (John 14:17 NIV). If you'd like to read more about the Holy Spirit, read John 14:15-31(NIV) and Acts 2 (NIV).

I reflect on my life quite a bit as I grow older. I have loved God since I was a young girl. I know I did because I wrote journals of poems and letters to Him. I believed in God and Jesus from an early age, but as I've shared, I didn't personally *know* Him or His heart because I didn't read the Bible. I certainly did not understand dying to my selfish desires and taking up my cross to live fully for Him. A good description of this concept comes from one of my favorite Bible teachers, Dr. David Jeremiah. This is how he explains it: "The Holy Spirit doesn't want to just be the resident of your life; He wants to be the president of your life."[XVI] My flesh was president of my life.

Dr. Austin Rogers notes in his book, *Ten Secrets for a Successful Family*[XVII] that flesh spelled backward is SELF without the H or Him (God). My "self," the self that Dr. Rogers was referring to, was alive and active. And I live with the consequences of those choices to this day. But I no longer live in guilt and shame thanks to Jesus and the Holy Spirit reminding me of Truth.

We either live by the flesh or the Spirit. And as Pastor Tyson Coughlin said in one of his teachings, the struggle between the two is evidence of the Holy Spirit within us, wanting to lead us on the path of life and protection. Romans 12:2 (NIV) advises, "Do not conform to the pattern of this world, but be transformed by the renewing of your mind. Then you will be able to test and approve what God's will is—his good, pleasing and perfect will."

We are either conformed (flesh) or transformed (Spirit). Which nature are you feeding? I've shared which one I was feeding.

> [16]So I say, walk by the Spirit, and you will not gratify the desires of the flesh. [17]For the flesh desires what is contrary to the Spirit, and the Spirit what is contrary to the flesh. They are in conflict with each other, so that you are not to do whatever you want. [18]But if you are led by the Spirit, you are not under the law.
>
> [19]The acts of the flesh are obvious: sexual immorality, impurity and debauchery; [20]idolatry and witchcraft; hatred, discord, jealousy, fits of rage, selfish ambition, dissensions, factions [21]and envy; drunkenness, orgies, and the like. I warn you, as I did before, that those who live like this will not inherit the kingdom of God."
> (Galatians 5:16-21 NIV)

It is possible to believe in Jesus without living a Holy Spirit-filled life. That was me. It was only when I started reading the Bible and asking God to reveal Himself to me that the Spirit convicted me of my sin of abortion, and I had a desire to repent. Note that I *asked.* God gives us free will. He will never force anything. We have to want to listen. Now I know that I repressed the Spirit so much that I couldn't even hear His Voice.

We must live Spirit-minded—full of love, joy, and peace. "For the kingdom of God is not a matter of eating or drinking, but of righteousness, peace and joy in the Holy Spirit" (Romans 14:17 NIV).

What is the answer to sin? Love. This is life in the Spirit. Sin is death (abortion); love is life, and it is noted in Romans:

> 8Let no debt remain outstanding, except the continuing debt to love one another, for whoever loves others has fulfilled the law. 9The commandments, "You shall not commit adultery," "You shall not murder," "You shall not steal," "You shall not covet," and whatever other command there may be, are summed up in this one command: "Love your neighbor as yourself." 10Love does no harm to a neighbor. Therefore love is the fulfillment of the law. (Romans 13:8-10 NIV)

Jesus was the fulfillment of the law in the Old Testament. He is pure love and dwells in us when we are saved. Dying to our selfish desires is impossible without the help of the Holy Spirit. Actually, much of what I've written in this book from my baka season and beyond was the Holy Spirit speaking and working in me. We must *seek*—a verb that means we are actively pursuing Jesus. He is waiting. And we must see and hear with our spiritual heart; the flesh is dead and not of help in spiritual things. We cannot do any of this apart from God's help, which is where abiding is crucial in our relationship with Him. John 15 (NIV) addresses this if you'd like to know more.

This may sound like I am preaching, especially if you are not a Believer or a baby Christian, but I don't want you to miss out on what a life led by the Holy Spirit can mean. I don't want you to live with a dry, shallow faith like I did for half my life. Find a circle of friends growing in God. Find a solid Bible-teaching church. Get connected at church. Find friends who pray with you and for you. Abundant life is what He desires for you and me! Contend for it. "It is for freedom that Christ has set us free. Stand firm, then, and do not let yourselves be burdened again by a yoke of slavery" (Galatians 5:1 NIV). Stand firm. Don't ever forget it's for *freedom* that Christ has set us free.

Song to stream:

Hillsong Worship. "This I Believe" (The Creed). Track 3, *No Other Name*. Hillsong Music and Resources LLC, 2014, available as a digital download.

Psalm 66:16-20 NIV

[16]"Come and hear, all you who fear God;
let me tell you what he has done for me.

[17] I cried out to him with my mouth;
his praise was on my tongue.

[18] If I had cherished sin in my heart,
the Lord would not have listened;

[19] but God has surely listened
and has heard my prayer.

[20] Praise be to God,
who has not rejected my prayer
or withheld his love from me!"

9 / grace, pure grace

"Let us then approach God's throne of grace with
confidence, so that we may receive mercy and find grace to
help us in our time of need."
—Hebrews 4:16 (NIV)

I'D DO ANYTHING to erase my abortion. I wish I could
tell my younger self to get a Bible, read it, and be on guard.
I'd do anything to take it all back and change the outcome.

Our baby girl would be thirty-four right now, and our
living children would have an older sister. We would know
her personality, see the features in her face, watch her use her
talents in the world, and perhaps watch her fall in love, get
married, and have her own family. Our parents would have
another grandchild, and we may have more grandchildren.

As much as I'd like to make it all go away, I also realize
God has used the experience to shape me into who I am
today. If I am a beloved child of God, made in His image,
accepted by Him, lavished by His love and forgiveness, then
I am called to love myself because God loves me. He thinks

the same of you. When He looks at you and me, he sees Jesus now. And honestly, *nothing* else matters. I love this quote by Dr. Caroline Leaf, "We can't shame ourselves into change. You can only love yourself into healing." God's love for us is enough to love ourselves.

I wish I could erase it. I can't, but guess what, *God has*. This is grace, pure grace. It's a gift from God that can be hard to comprehend, but we must accept it to grasp His goodness and live in freedom fully. And then, we must *live* as if we believe it. We don't earn or deserve His grace. It's a gift. It's Him looking at my abortion, and yours, and saying, "I don't remember that anymore." So, He asks, "Why do you keep bringing that up? I don't even remember that. When you repented, it was erased." I know this from Psalm 103:11-12 (NIV), which says, "¹¹For as high as the heavens are above the earth, so great is his love for those who fear him; ¹²as far as the east is from the west, so far has he removed our transgressions from us."

With that said, I know what we think of ourselves can be a serious struggle. I have struggled at times, too, especially when I was waking up to the truth of my abortion. Sometimes it still haunts me when I take my eyes off Jesus. The enemy of our souls loves to keep people tangled up in guilt and shame, especially when they have been in relationships where they always had to give something to receive something. With all I am, I pray you *receive* this grace from God with no strings attached. It's not a negotiation based on your good work; it's freely given, as noted in Romans 11:6 (NIV), "And if by grace, then it cannot be based on works; otherwise, grace would no longer be grace."

It is okay to have an honest talk with the Lord about your struggles. He already knows them, but He desperately wants you to talk with Him about it and ask others to pray for you. Remember how the God of all creation thinks of you. There is no opinion more important than His. We will overcome by renewing our minds daily with the truth of His Word. It will be very difficult for us to live by the Spirit (president) and not the flesh (resident) if we let the world define us, or if we let people around us, who don't know Jesus, speak to who we are.

Recently, a friend gave me an extremely nice, totally unexpected gift. It wasn't Christmas or a holiday where gift exchanges are expected, but a random weekday. And it was a really nice gift.

At first, I wanted to run out and get her something in return. Then, I realized that it was a blessing *to her* to give me the gift. I realized I didn't want to take away the feeling of being blessed from her. Instead, I wanted to accept the love she had for me that made her want to give me that gift, completely unwarranted or unsolicited. It was from her heart, just like the free, undeserved gift of grace from God's heart to you.

Grace is a gift that isn't earned. It's the exchange of a gift instead of punishment, even though we messed up. "My grace is sufficient for you, for my power is made perfect in weakness" (2 Corinthians 12:9 NIV).

God *is* grace. Otherwise, why would a Holy God want to be reconciled to us, sinners? As we continue to embrace this truth and accept it fully, it's important to remember that our salvation is by God's grace alone. Salvation is the most supreme illustration of grace. We could never earn it, and we are reminded, in Romans 5:8 (NIV), that He died for us while we were still sinners: "But God demonstrates his own love for us in this: While we were still sinners, Christ died for us." And, in Ephesians 2:8-9 (NIV), the Bible expands on this point, "⁸For it is by grace you have been saved, through faith—and this is not from yourselves, it is the gift of God—⁹not by works, so that no one can boast."

I have some awesome Jesus sisters. I've shared how important community is for healing (and living life supported), so I thank Him often for these friends. I asked some of them to share their thoughts, feelings, examples, and stories on grace. If you aren't familiar with God's grace, I hope one or more of these will help you understand what it can look and feel like.

†

GRACE is an acronym for God's Riches At Christ's Expense (GRACE).

GRACE is uttering gratitude for all the times I have failed Him and others, and He picked me up and gave me the strength to forgive myself and grow stronger.

GRACE is when my kids used to do something wrong, and they begged for "grace." It would mean that they did not get what they deserved. It would mean love outweighs punishment. But the lessons were learned gently. I taught them about the Lord's grace.

GRACE is forgiveness of our sins and also all the blessings He gives us that we don't deserve—like adoption, becoming heirs, receiving the Holy Spirit, spiritual gifts, understanding of the Word—GRACE upon GRACE.

GRACE is when I'm not staying in the Word or in communication with Him, but He is always there for me when I come back.

GRACE is a gift that isn't earned. It's the exchange of a gift instead of punishment, even though we missed the mark or messed up. "My grace is sufficient for you" (2 Corinthians 12:9 NIV) is a form of supernatural resilience.

His GRACE is a gift to me. It's true love. By GRACE we are saved through faith. I am seen by Him as if I had never sinned (justified).

GRACE is God's power in us that is enough to overcome every weakness we have. That's grace.

GRACE is Jesus on the Cross asking God to forgive those crucifying Him because "they didn't know what they were doing."

GRACE is Jesus forgiving Peter, who denied knowing him three times, then appearing to Peter after His resurrection and preparing breakfast for him.

GRACE is taking a friend to lunch after she has talked badly about you to another friend because she is hurt from past wounds and not healed. GRACE is loving her through her pain and your pain.

GRACE is running from God your whole life, then realizing He is all you need, and He welcomes you with open arms.

GRACE is the story of a drunk driver who killed his best friend, who was an only child. From the moment his mother saw the drunk driver after the accident, to the trial, to today, she hugs him, says she loves him, and kisses him. Her request to the judge for a pardon during the trial prevented him from spending the rest of his life in jail. In his words, "She saved my life for taking her only son's life."

✝

For me personally, GRACE is God gifting us three living children after we aborted our first child. God's grace is greater than our sin.

Song to stream:

Chris Tomlin. "Amazing Grace." Track 12, *See the Morning.* EMI Christian Music Group, 2006, worship hymn with updated lyrics.

10 / *from stuttering to singing*

"The place of our greatest warfare is the place
of our greatest inheritance."
—*Marti Pieper*

DO YOU KNOW the story of my good friend Moses in the Bible? You can get to know him beginning with the second chapter of Exodus, the second book of the Bible. He was just like me—and maybe you, too. He doubted himself, not believing he could do what God asked of him, which was to lead the Israelites out of Egyptian slavery to the Promised Land for freedom.

Moses was believed to have a stutter, which made God's request even more intimidating for him. "Pardon your servant, Lord. I have never been eloquent, neither in the past nor since you have spoken to your servant. I am slow of speech and tongue" (Exodus 4:10 NIV).

So, if he was slow of speech and tongue, how could he be the leader of a large group of people and do what God asked of him? His self-doubt and fear are understandable and relatable. It was a monumental ask.

The parallel I want to draw here is that my healing stuttered at the beginning, like Moses's speech, or like a campfire that takes time to get going. It would have been easier to abandon the work that healing would require, but then I would've missed the abundant life Christ yearned for me to have.

I love Moses' story. I can relate to him all day long. As a mom, I have repeatedly doubted my parenting. But, as I've grown in my relationship with Jesus, I've become more confident because His Word teaches and equips me to parent. In my professional life as an entrepreneur, there have been countless times that I have doubted myself and wanted to run the other way. If I had, I wouldn't have allowed God to show His power in my weakness and have the flexibility I have today.

I've also never doubted myself as much as I have while writing this book. I can't help but wonder, *Is it even good? Will it help women and men?* As I write, I remind myself that if I don't release the doubts and let God use them as He wants, I will miss the opportunity and the blessings that come from obedience to Him. It's all a journey of reliance and trust. God has a lot to teach us, but we must be willing to move from where we are to see His faithfulness and receive His healing. You may be stuttering still (stuck in shame, guilt, and darkness—your heart barely puttering toward healing)—but, like Moses, I believe your singing is coming.

Moses did everything he could to avoid his assignment from God. He even said, "O Lord, please send someone else to do it" (Exodus 4:13 NIV). Eventually, he reluctantly obeyed, and, in a way, it turned out to be his healing, too. Moses became the leader of God's people, but only after his parents surrendered him because he was a Hebrew baby born in Egypt. Pharaoh demanded that all newborn Hebrew baby boys be killed. After concealing him for three months, his mother realized she could not protect him and made the difficult decision to put him in a basket to float away down the river. The daughter of Pharaoh found him, and Moses became her son.

Once he was an adult, Moses saw an Egyptian beating a Hebrew slave, and he killed the Egyptian. He then fled to the desert, away from Pharaoh, and became a shepherd. This is where the Lord spoke to him through a burning bush, telling him to return to Egypt to lead the Israelites out of slavery. God performed a series of miracles to free the Hebrews from the Egyptians with Moses as their leader. Ultimately, God parted the Red Sea for their final escape.

After the parting of the Red Sea, the Israelites wandered in the desert for forty years (because of grumbling and disobedience), on their way to the land God promised. But because of his disobedience, Moses never saw the Promised Land. His story is one to behold because of his unwavering trust in the Lord. Despite overwhelming burdens and numerous setbacks, Moses continually sought the Lord's presence and trusted Him. Because of this, he also had deep intimacy with Him.

I wanted to share Moses's story because it mirrors mine— and can be yours, too. Moses told God every reason he could not do what He asked, but by the end of Moses' life, after clinging to Him for many years through trials, he sang! Imagine the stutterer now *singing*, "³I will proclaim the name of the Lord. Oh, praise the greatness of our God! ⁴He is the Rock, his works are perfect, and all his ways are just. A faithful God who does no wrong, upright and just is he," Moses's song in Deuteronomy 32:3-4 (NIV).

My soul sings today, and I have written this book for one reason—to lead you to the One True God who wants you to sing, too. I've shared that when I realized the truth of our abortion and how heinous it was, I lived under a debilitating weight. I felt so alone in my filth. I felt as if I couldn't tell a soul. It's such a disgusting truth, and I didn't want anyone to know. As I've already shared, I knew what it felt like to be silent and for my bones to waste away, groaning all day long, as described in Psalm 32:3 (NIV).

Hopefully, you realize by now it wasn't until I chose to dive into reading the Bible and get to know God's tender heart that I could start to breathe again. God took my hand very gently and walked with me. It took years, but the small steps and stuttering in my soul eventually became singing. I experienced joy and freedom, finally living without guilt or shame. I believe God is doing the same for you right now. He is a *gentle*man. He will never force anyone to walk with Him.

Please accept this book as your invitation to *know* Him through *His book*. There is nothing He wants more than to take you from stuttering to singing—your heart singing every day because of what He has done for you, as said in the book

of Matthew, "²⁸Come to me, all you who are weary and burdened, and I will give you rest. ²⁹Take my yoke upon you,
and learn from me, for I am gentle and humble in heart, and
you will find rest for your souls. ³⁰For my yoke is easy and my
burden is light" (Matthew 11:28-30 NIV).

In chapter seven, I listed very specific habits I have imple-
mented in my life to live victorious in Christ. Those habits
and daily disciplines freed me from guilt and shame, enabling
me to live in freedom and joy today. They will always be part
of my weekly rhythm. For my soul to sing again, there was
one more choice I had to make that was quite possibly the
hardest of them all—I had to choose to stop mourning my
aborted baby.

This may sound completely coldhearted and inconsistent,
but remember the title of my book is "*the soul's hole.*" Because
in my experience, that hole never goes away. The Lord has
healed me, but I will never avoid the consequences of my
decision—sadness and regret. The key is to stop *dwelling* on
what has been forgiven. We must accept our choice, move
on, and believe the promises God has given us in His Word.
Believing these Truths means living them out and choosing
to apply them to our everyday lives. Mourning too long puts
a fog over our future and keeps us from being free. It prevents
God from using us as new creatures in Him.

When I reflect on my story, I always think of King David
in the Bible because he sinned, repented, and was forgiven,
but his life was never the same. David was called "a man
after God's own heart" in 1 Samuel 13:14 (NIV) and in
Acts 13:22 (NIV). I'm not sure there could be a higher

the soul's hole / 108

compliment. God called him that, while He also knew his future sins against Him.

David failed terribly when he had an affair with Bathsheba, then later had her husband killed to avoid being caught. David was remorseful and repentant, and God forgave him. God still used David in mighty ways. Although David was forgiven and scripture implies that he was never separated from God because of his sincere repentance, he couldn't escape the consequences of his sin [See 2 Samuel 12:1-15 (NIV)]. God forgives, but there are consequences for our actions, which in my life have been deep sadness and regret.

We can't escape consequences, but we can choose to stop living in mourning and move forward. There is a beautiful example of mourning too long in the Old Testament when Samuel mourned Saul for too long: "The LORD said to Samuel, 'How long will you mourn for Saul, since I have rejected him as king over Israel? Fill your horn with oil and be on your way' " (1 Samuel 16:1 NIV).

Moving forward doesn't mean we will forget our child or stop loving them. It doesn't mean we don't regret what we did or stop wishing we could change it. It doesn't mean we don't cherish the baby's life or love them with all our hearts. It doesn't even mean we don't sob when we think of them. (I still do.)

In fact, all those feelings mean we are truly repentant. It means we now understand that the blood of Jesus covers us. God no longer thinks of our sin. If He doesn't, then we don't need to dwell on it either. We can't live in joy if we stay in the past. We must "fill our horn (heart) with oil" (the Holy Spirit) and "be on our way" like the Lord told Samuel.

I love what Pastor Dr. David Jeremiah says about babies and children in heaven in his book, *Revealing the Mysteries of Heaven*. I hope this comforts you as much as it has me. He said:

> If He is good to all, that would surely include infants; and if His tender mercies are over all His works, that would certainly include children. Abraham summed it up when he said, 'Shall not the Judge of all the earth do right?' (Genesis 18:25) God is fair and would never judge anyone unfairly or treat anyone without mercy. He knows, as we do, that babies cannot understand the witness of God, either in creation or in the Scripture. They cannot yet comprehend the truth of the Gospel. Yet God loves them deeply. He loves children, and He delights in the babies He has created. He loves the unborn.
>
> Until we reach a certain age, our hearts and minds cannot grasp the Gospel message. Such souls are protected under the blood of Christ. They are not sinless, as I said, for we've all inherited the sinful nature of our first parents, but they are described in the Bible as 'innocents,' and are, I believe, included in the redemptive power of the blood of the loving Savior.[XVIII]

I genuinely believe that we will see our babies again one day. They are safe and happy with Jesus until we are with them again (if we have salvation in Jesus).

I hesitate to share this, especially if you are a new believer or a "baby Christian," but I know it's very important and needs to be said. There is an invisible war between good and evil all around us. As believers, we are united to God in Christ by the Holy Spirit, but there is an adversary called Satan who *does not* want you to be set free by the blood of Jesus. He will do absolutely everything to keep you in bondage.

I want you to be aware of him when you are struggling spiritually, emotionally, mentally, and physically. The Bible says he prowls around like a lion looking for someone to devour. He aims to kill, steal, and destroy. The last thing I want is for you to think staying in shame and guilt would be better than knowing the freedom and joy in Jesus. That's the farthest thing from the truth. Our God is so much greater!

God doesn't leave us helpless. He gives us His armor to "put on" every day to fight the enemy:

> [10]Finally, be strong in the Lord and in his mighty power. [11]Put on the full armor of God, so that you can take your stand against the devil's schemes. [12]For our struggle is not against flesh and blood, but against the rulers, against the authorities, against the powers of this dark world and against the spiritual forces of evil in the heavenly realms. [13]Therefore put on the full armor of God, so that when the day of evil comes, you may be able to stand your ground, and after you have done everything, to stand. [14]Stand firm then, with the belt of truth buckled around your waist, with the breastplate of righteousness in place, [15]and with your feet fitted with the readiness that comes

from the gospel of peace. [16]In addition to all this, take up the shield of faith, with which you can extinguish all the flaming arrows of the evil one. [17]Take the helmet of salvation and the sword of the Spirit, which is the word of God. (Ephesians 6:10-17 NIV)

While writing this book, the level of spiritual warfare I experienced was unprecedented in my life. The enemy tried very hard to keep me from finishing this book, and he tried to make me doubt everything I believe. Now I see it clearly—of course, it was warfare. I am a threat to the devil because he doesn't want you to be set free by the Blood of the Lamb and the word of my testimony. He wants all of us trapped in a swirling hole of torment, guilt, eternal destruction, and self-hatred. This attack lasted for months and felt relentless. The enemy made me doubt absolutely everything I believe, which felt like torture, because in Whom I believe is absolutely everything I am today. These were never-ending thoughts trying to make me doubt the life of Jesus, His death, and His resurrection. There were many days when I was tormented by these thoughts that stalled my writing, sometimes for months.

But God showed me how to win the battle, in my mind, by putting on His armor every single day. Instead of being embarrassed (which my flesh wanted to do), I asked my prayer sisters to pray for me. I worshipped Him and gave thanks through it all. I prayed scripture out loud. I also dug into books and podcasts proving the life and resurrection of Christ. The coolest part of this was that what the enemy meant for harm, God truly used for my good. Because of this struggle, my belief and faith are stronger than ever.

During this tough time, the Lord used another very ordinary, tangible moment to help me. I was in the Indianapolis airport in April 2024, wearing an American Idol t-shirt and asking people to vote for our son, Blake, who made the top twenty-four that season.

God literally used that t-shirt to introduce me to a special new friend, Renee Swope. She asked me if I was Blake's mom, which started an awesome conversation about our lives. I found out quickly that she was an author and loved Jesus, too. The following week, we talked on the phone for more than an hour about my book and her experience writing her books. God knew I needed her on this final stretch of intense warfare. Renee warfare-prayed over me and held me accountable for writing a certain number of words each week. He used her to help me finish writing. She mentored, coached, and encouraged me, believing that the world needs to hear my story. God used her to help me sing again and get back to writing!

The devil doesn't mess with people who are not about God's business. He likes it when we are "in the middle"— lukewarm as the Bible describes it. Once we've taken God's side, it's game on.

A dear friend once told me that the devil's voice will get louder as you get closer to your calling. (Thank you, Kathrine) In our case, this means healing. So, stay strong in the Lord. I hope this shows you how personal God is in each of our lives.

His hand is all over everything if we cry out to Him and stay close to Him in our struggles.

Let's talk about joy as we finish our journey together. Joy is one of my favorite words. No one wants you to feel true joy more than the Lord. As I've gotten older, I've realized that joy isn't an emotion when it comes from God. It is supernatural and it's a spiritual blessing, because it's a fruit of the Spirit. Jesus says, "As the father has loved me, so have I loved you. Now remain in my love. If you keep my commands, you will remain in my love, just as I have kept my Father's commands and remain in his love. I have told you this so that my joy may be in you and that your joy may be complete" (John 15:9 NIV).

Joy comes from remaining in God's love by keeping his commands. It lives in the depths of our soul, coming from knowing Jesus personally and intimately. It comes from worship, thanksgiving, and repentance. It comes from walking with him day in and day out, even when things are hard and don't make sense. It comes through a community that loves Jesus, too. It comes with rescue. It comes with forgiveness by the Eternal, the God of the universe, who did everything He needed to bring us back to Himself. It is complete in Jesus, and this true joy will make us want to sing again!

Here is more beautiful scripture about joy and singing:

"And those the Lord has rescued will return. They will enter Zion with singing; everlasting joy will crown their heads. Gladness and joy will overtake them, and sorrow and sighing will flee away." (Isaiah 35:10 NIV).

"You make known to me the path of life; you will fill me with joy in your presence, with eternal pleasures at your right hand" (Psalm 16:11 NIV).

[11]"You turned my wailing into dancing; you removed my sackcloth and clothed me with joy,
[12]that my heart may sing your praises and not be silent. Lord my God, I will praise you forever" (Psalm 30:11-12 NIV).

I want to reach through these pages and hug you. This isn't easy work, but it's the most important work of your life. And you're not alone because God carries the heaviest load. He needs you to lay it all down at the Cross and partner with Him on the journey. I wish we could hang out and take a long walk together. You are brave and ready to heal. I'm your biggest cheerleader and prayer sister.

God has one last thing to say to you: " 'Come now, let us settle the matter,' says the Lord. 'Though your sins are like scarlet, they shall be as white as snow; though they are red as crimson, they shall be like wool' " (Isaiah 1:18 NIV).

The matter is settled. Go in peace and freedom.

Song to stream:

John Wilds. "Worthy." *We Fall Down (live)*. John Wilds and Bethel Music, 2025, All digital formats.

ADDITIONAL ABORTION STORIES

THE FOLLOWING PAGES are filled with personal abortion stories by women who care about you as much as I do. A few have had multiple abortions, and one was raped and chose life. By sharing these stories, I hope to continue showing the power of a life surrendered to Jesus.

If you can't identify with my story, then maybe their stories will feel more like yours. Over the years, God has used their bravery to strengthen me. I pray they strengthen you, too, and show you that you are not alone.

Leigh's Story

As I sit in my favorite coffee shop listening to the worship song "My Lighthouse," my heart is full. When you hear my story, you might wonder, "How can you say that?" Well, the tremendous joy and redemption that my Lord and Savior has given me through the pain, blame, guilt, anger, and total feeling of helplessness reassure me that He is my lighthouse.

I am going to start my story with this: You are an overcomer with Jesus, but you have to allow him to lead you up and out of the trenches where the devil has held you.

My journey started when I was fifteen years old. I had just started my sophomore year of high school. I was a cheerleader and in a relationship with a boy who was a year older than me. I was in love (or so I thought) and, in my mind, if you loved someone, it was okay to engage in a sexual relationship.

As a fifteen-year-old girl who did not know Jesus personally, I was the perfect target for Satan. I had no idea how certain choices would affect my future, but boy, did they.

I remember it vividly. It was in August, and I was in a panic. I always started my period by the fifth of the month, and well... no period. All I remember thinking was, *This can't be happening! What am I going to do?*

You see, my parents felt very strongly that people should not have sex before marriage, and I knew they would be so disappointed. Here I was, facing the reality of my choices.

Time seemed to stop that day as I sat in the dark, all alone, waiting for those results! I remember seeing those pink lines, and I could not breathe. The fear was overwhelming! That is the day my nightmare began—or so I thought.

Although I did not know it then, there was a war going on around me, and Satan, so cunningly, began to convince me that the only choice I had was to have this baby terminated. *Me?* What? Was this real? I suddenly began to feel as if I was watching my life on a movie screen.

Before I continue, I want to ask you something. Do you believe in good versus evil?

I am here to tell you that they are both very real. Satan is a master at making something bad seem good. He is the master manipulator. He is also the author of fear, confusion, and doubt.

I mustered up the courage to call my boyfriend, and when I told him that I was pregnant, there was silence on the other end of the phone. I began to cry. This was the moment my feelings went numb.

The next five years began a downward spiral where I allowed Satan to blind me spiritually, emotionally, and mentally in all decisions, resulting in five abortions.

As I write this, all the emotions flood back at me. I can see the room, I can smell the sterile smell of the alcohol and formaldehyde, and I can see the tray of utensils that would be used to end my baby's life. I remember the nurse coming into the room and giving me the gown to change into, and telling me to get undressed and lie on the table.

The doctor came in and said I would feel a pinch to numb the area inside, and then pressure. As I lay there, I began to hear a vacuum suction. I tried to ignore the sound, but it was deafening. The cramping was beyond any I had experienced before.

Then, everything stopped. The nurse came over and told me I could get up and get dressed. She gave me a large pad to put in my underwear because she said I would probably experience cramping and a heavy period. I paid them and waited for my boyfriend in silence and complete numbness.

What goes through a woman's mind in this stage of this decision?

I had allowed Satan to convince me that the baby was the problem, and I was doing the responsible thing by not bringing an unplanned child into the world. With the "problem" gone, all would be fine.

It was not until 1997 that Jesus began to slowly draw me toward Him, and on May 4, 1997, I became a follower of Christ. That is when He radically changed me.

You see, He used my four beautiful children to point me to Him.

As I grew in my faith, Jesus began to speak to my heart about what I chose all those years ago. Even though I understood God's promise that my sins are now covered under the blood of Jesus, I was sure there was no way He would forgive me for taking the lives of five babies.

In His gentle way, Jesus began to reveal Satan's lies to me. He showed me that the reason I continually felt the need for physical validation (in the form of sexual intercourse) was that I had always felt ugly.

Jesus revealed that Satan started courting me when he saw how much it hurt to have others make fun of me. Satan found my weakness and capitalized on it—my physical appearance.

Since that day in May, I have learned to trust Jesus to use my mess as His message of redemption for others. He has reminded me so gently of how precious and beautiful I am in his eyes. There are no words to express the freedom I have in knowing my Lord and Savior does not see me as the person

I was, but instead, He sees me as His beloved child. I will be forever grateful!

Mindy's Story

My whole life was a quest for love or, more precisely, a quest to be loved. At age eight, my parents divorced, and my mom moved us across the country. Looking back, I recognize that I was suffering from severe depression.

I began skipping school, became very angry, and started cussing to relieve the pain. I often walked to school with my books held tightly to my chest, my head bowed, hiding the tears I couldn't control. I missed my dad, I was away from everything that I knew, and I felt very alone.

To add to the pain, I was sexually abused by an adult and friends. It led me to wonder what was wrong with me. There must be something wrong with me because people who are loved don't get treated this way. I must not be worthy. As I grew, it became almost an obsession to fill my heart with the love I needed.

To understand the desperation I felt, consider what starving children look like. Their eyes bulge, their ribs show, their bellies distend, and they wear an expression of emptiness. That is what I imagine my heart looked like. When you are depleted of something your body needs, you will do anything to satisfy it. I was willing to dig in the dumpsters of this world to find the love my heart craved. I was desperate.

Like many, I learned about love from television, soap operas, culture, and friends. The resounding message was,

"Love is found in sex." I bought that lie, and for many years into adulthood, I did what I was taught. I received temporary satisfaction in those moments before sex, when a man says all the right things. He is kind, gentle, and will give you the world, until you give him what he came for—then all bets are off. All promises are broken. However, desperation drove me to engage in this behavior even more.

Up to that point in my life, no man stayed. My dad wasn't consistent in my life, and all of my boyfriends quickly dumped me. So, when I was raped, I felt used in the vilest way. I no longer questioned if I was worthy of love; I knew I was not. After a quick inventory of my life, coupled with my definition of love, I began to take what I could get. Partying, bars, nightlife, and one-night stands were where I found love. I jumped in. It wasn't hard. I was already living that lifestyle; now, I lived it with gusto.

During my first pregnancy, I was no longer dating the father of the baby when I found out I was pregnant. My current boyfriend said it was either him or the baby. I chose him! He was willing to stay if I got rid of the baby, and he would help me pay for it. Someone loved me. After the abortion, I swore I would never do that again. I knew what pregnancy was, and it wasn't a clump of cells.

When I became pregnant a few months later, we decided to keep the baby. I would have it no other way. We ended up living in different states because he was in the military. During my pregnancy, he was kind and loving one day, distant and aloof the next. On the aloof days, he would tell me about the parties and girls in his life. On the good days, I was the only one he had eyes for, and he longed to be a daddy. Nine months of this, coupled with the hormones of pregnancy, had me on an emotional roller coaster. During labor, he continued playing his games. I was spent emotionally. We eventually broke up.

Now a single mom, I enrolled in college and met another man. We eventually moved into his home, but after a short time, we broke up, only to discover I was pregnant. He didn't want me, and he didn't want any more children. He paid for the abortion.

Afterward, when my daughter's father wanted to get back together, get married, and have more children, I was thrilled. I called him one evening to tell him the good news: I was pregnant! His response was, "I have to go eat dinner." I was devastated. The memories of my previous pregnancy with him came flooding back. There was no way I would survive another baby with him. Without telling anyone but the friend who drove me, I went to have a third abortion.

A new question formulated in my mind: "What person of any worth does this to their children?" For the next several years, despite my revelation, I went back to the garbage pits of this world; In my mind, I was not worth any more than that.

And then came Jesus.

I began to read the Bible. I started to hope. One Sunday morning, while attending church, I accepted the truth. Jesus saved me. For all those years, far back in the recesses of my mind, I longed for true love. I longed to be accepted, validated for who I was, not for what I had to offer. I kept those thoughts deep in my mind; I dared not hope.

But this Sunday morning, hope was in the name of Jesus, and it became real to me. I quickly joined prayer groups and Bible studies. I began reading my Bible and books about the names of God. Yet, there was still doubt. On my bed at night, I heard these words, "God can't love you because you killed His kids," and "Those people are not like you; they will never understand you." After a few months of this, I left the church.

I didn't grow up in the church. I had no context for anything Christian. I believed in God, but He was a god of my making. So, when I would lie on my bed and hear those awful accusations, I didn't understand that they were truths mixed with lies. I had never heard of spiritual warfare, grace, or that we are equal at the cross. It never occurred to me that I had weapons of warfare to fight with. I believed I was the only one with a past like mine. I thought no one had ever made the choices I made. I believed the lie.

Facing rejection from people I enjoyed being around was too much to bear. Being rejected by God wasn't something I wanted to experience, so I walked away. I went back to my old ways. I had been comfortable in that lifestyle because it was familiar, and I knew what to expect. However, it was like a dog returning to its vomit. I had tasted the Lord; His word was like honey on my lips. So, returning to my old ways turned out to be vile and disgusting. It was no longer comfortable; I was out of place.

I would one day learn how God leaves the ninety-nine to search for the one. I spent a year trying to live my old life.

Looking back, I can see how God was pursuing me, chasing after His beloved and wooing my heart. During this time, my desire to know more about this God who saved me began to grow.

I finally broke from my past and began the journey of walking with God. It took years before I completely stopped some of my past behaviors. I needed time to learn about God, to be surrounded by loving Christians, and to learn what it meant to be a believer in Christ. Learning what it means to truly love can only be taught by God, and sometimes it takes time. God, the Lover of my soul, was patient and persistent. He was kind and tender to teach me, lead me, and show me that His love was displayed on the cross. He bore my stripes. He took my place. He delivered me because He delighted in me. God loves me!

God's love is eternal, authentic, and everlasting. He loves me because it is who He is. His love is unfailing!

Amy's Story

At sixteen, I found myself pregnant. I was raised in a Christian home by a family that was deeply involved in the church. I knew this would bring shame on them in their community and among our family members. So, when my boyfriend said, "We are going to get an abortion," I went along with it, thinking it would solve my problem and allow me to go on with my life as usual. I trusted my boyfriend, but I knew this was a way to cover up my sin.

Also, no one ever told me that abortion was wrong, that it was killing a baby, not my parents or my youth pastor. In fact, the world was telling me the opposite. It was okay. It was not a baby, but rather just tissue, a clump of cells. After all, it was a legal choice, so it must be okay, right?

Instead of being the solution, abortion left me deeply traumatized. I don't remember a lot from that day; however, I do remember how the doctor made me feel. He never looked at me or even spoke a word to me. I remember he grabbed my ankles and put them in the stirrups. I remember the sound of the suction. When I left the clinic that day, I was no longer the same girl who walked in. Before the abortion, I was a thriving, normal sixteen-year-old girl. I was an A/B student in high school, had fun with family and friends, enjoyed my youth group at church, and was generally a happy teen. After the abortion, I began skipping school, and my grades plummeted. I refused to attend church or family functions and would only hang out with my party friends. I went from smoking weed very seldom to saying yes to every drug offered. I just wanted to forget about the abortion. I wanted to numb the pain. I wanted to silence the voices in my head. I wanted to stop the flashbacks.

I was horrible to my parents—belligerent, rebellious, inconsiderate, hateful. I lied to them and about them. I stole from them, and I manipulated them. I was horrible to my sisters. My oldest sister and I developed a very hostile relationship. My actions devastated the family. And I did not realize it at the time. Frankly, I did not care. I was in a downward spiral. My behavior was so reckless because, in my mental state, I did not care if I lived or died. Self-loathing and suicidal thoughts were swirling daily, and I could only find relief in drugs and alcohol.

I did not realize it then, but I left that clinic with a wound. I was confused. Abortion was supposed to be a solution where nobody got hurt. Obviously, that was a big lie.

That lie caused so much pain and anger that I started down a road of self-destruction. I cared about nothing but coping with my pain and anger. I tried it all—drugs, alcohol, and promiscuity, which led to another pregnancy and another abortion. Looking back on that time now, I can see that I was punishing myself for choosing to kill my babies. I often thought of suicide and believed I deserved to die.

For the next three years, there were many counselors—although I would refuse to see them. There were multiple arrests and court dates, as well as a drug recovery program. There were school suspensions, summer school, and an alternative school. I barely graduated from high school in 1986.

All this time, I knew God was there, watching over me. I could feel Him, and I'm certain I would not be here today if He had not protected me in many of the compromising situations I put myself in. Despite this, I felt so ashamed of my choices that I didn't feel worthy to go to Him for help. I was certain I deserved absolutely nothing, unless it was misery and pain.

At nineteen, I found myself pregnant for the third time and chose to carry. Zachary will be thirty-three this month, and I tell him he saved my life. But really, it was God, right? God had been there all along, right beside me during those years my heart was crying out. My relationship with Him grew, and I asked for forgiveness for my choice to abort. Of course, He forgave me. 1 John 1:9 says, "If we confess our sins, He is faithful and just and will forgive us our sins and purify us from all unrighteousness."

The drug and alcohol abuse stopped, but the mental struggles continued. The anxiety, depression, suicidal thoughts, flashbacks, triggers, self-punishing behaviors, and self-hate continued to varying degrees for the next thirty years.

In 2017, I heard of an abortion recovery group at my church and immediately knew I needed it. At last, there seemed to be hope for my wounded heart. This group helped me understand what I had been experiencing mentally and emotionally from the trauma of my choice. This group helped me resolve the pain and anger using God's word. Most importantly, this group helped me learn how to forgive myself. You see, I knew God had forgiven me for my abortion, but my prison was in not forgiving myself. I spent thirty years not forgiving myself, decades of believing the lies the enemy was telling me: "You're worthless. You will never be a good mom. People would hate you if they knew what you did. You don't deserve anything good. You should just end it now." But God had other plans for me! He had plans for me to prosper, not harm me, plans to give me hope and a future! Once God showed me how to forgive myself, it was like the cage opened. I was no longer a prisoner to those toxic thoughts and behaviors.

My family relationships healed. I apologized to my parents and sisters for all the dysfunction and hurt I caused. My relationship with my oldest sister is the best it has ever been. My marriage has never been stronger as I am living in a healthy mental state, and my kids and I have very open, honest conversations about hard things. I recognized my codependency and no longer feel the need to control all outcomes. They have all told me how proud they are of me.

Today, I lead that abortion recovery group. What God did for me—I get to pay forward. I am no longer used by pain but rather use my pain to help others to bring glory to God. I never imagined that the girl with toxic thoughts and self-loathing could actually help someone with their mental health, but here I am!

The two recovery groups I lead every year help me stay mentally healthy. Quiet time and prayer with the Lord are necessities for me, as is Bible study. I also like "I am" statements and focused reflection. Every day, I CHOOSE to have a controlled, thoughtful life. God's Word is vital to my healthy mental state.

We all have ghosts in our past, broken dreams, desperation, failures, struggles. We all have hills and valleys. Let's not focus on the valleys, but rather the hills we are on today. As the lyrics of one of my favorite songs, "Redeemed" by Big Daddy Weave, say:

> I don't have to be the old man inside of me
> 'cause his day is long dead and gone
> I've got a new name, a new life, I'm not the same
> And a hope that will carry me home
> I am REDEEMED.

Song to stream:

Big Daddy Weave. "Redeemed." Track 7, *Love Come to Life: The Redeemed Edition*, Fervent Records/Spirit-Led, 2014. All digital formats.

Keyah's Story

I had never done research or heard about abortion before I got pregnant. I was made to believe that an abortion was my only choice when, in reality, I had the power to make the decision to keep my baby, but my voice had not yet been empowered. I was also significantly affected by what wasn't said. All of the pain and hurt I experience today comes from what wasn't said, like how the abortion would have such long-term effects on my mental state and lead to poor decision-making in relationships.

Mainly, I had an abortion because I was fifteen, and my parents said that it was the only choice. I didn't have anyone in my corner. My boyfriend left for the Navy, and all my relatives lived more than two hours away. Our reputation as a family had been built from the ground up since my family wasn't originally from our city.

It was a small city where everyone knew everyone. I think my parents' decision for me to have an abortion had a lot to do with upholding a positive image in the community. I was raised with an iron fist, so saying "No" to my parents wasn't an option.

In high school, I was ashamed about having an abortion, so I didn't tell my closest friends. I only shared it with one person, and it was only because she told me about her miscarriage. It wasn't until I went to college that I told my friends this "secret." I was able to speak freely about it after that because I saw that people weren't looking at me negatively.

Later in life, every time I drank too much alcohol, I became extremely sad, and my past abortion always became the topic of morbid conversation. It wasn't until then that I realized that I may still be secretly dealing with the hurt and pain from years past.

The drinking continued until 2018 when I decided to put the bottle down and tackle my issues head-on by getting involved with Embrace Grace, an Abortion Recovery group, Sidewalk Advocacy, and Triad Coalition for Life (all in Greensboro, North Carolina). I also decided that I deeply needed personal counseling for my family and me to heal. We have made so much progress toward a healthier relationship.

The guilt and shame hindered my relationship with my parents a great deal. I still don't feel that I can love them as they deserve, because there was a breach of trust that can never be fully repaired. With God, I can love them better than before, but I am only human, and only God can fix what is broken. It is His job to restore, and I believe it will be so here on Earth.

Drinking and partying had their own set of consequences. God saved my life several times, more times than I can coherently remember.

When I committed to stop drinking and smoking in 2018, God instantly honored my motion to save my life by removing any urge or thought to drink or smoke. I haven't looked back since.

I thought it was something that I could never be free of, but it turns out, it didn't have a hold on me; rather, I was holding on to it. When I let go and let God, everything unlike Him ceased. I had to do a lot on my part, though.

I cut off friends and got rid of inappropriate pieces of my wardrobe. I removed many secular songs from my playlists. Straight and narrow is the path for someone like me because I've come such a long way... too far to turn back now. He even gave me a disgust for the smell of smoke and liquor. I don't even want to be around it!

What I have learned is that you can never think the fight is over. I can't become complacent with my progress. That's when Satan sneaks back, and before you know it, you are back on that slippery slope. I have to keep my heart protected and filled with His Word. I must keep my eye gate closed to TV, social media, books, and other media sources that try to exalt themselves above what I know to be true in God's Word (which is His Will and His Way). I know I must keep my mouth away from gossip and instead cling to positive, uplifting speech, and keep my mind centered, grounded, and focused on helping others. When I serve others in God's name, He will honor the desires of my heart to do His will.

Teresa's Story

During my senior year in high school, I was dating a young man with whom I thought I was in love. He was a sweet guy. He was handsome, with big blue eyes! He was the first person I ever had sex with. Sex education was taught at my school, but I was just too immature to process what to do with the information. So, at seventeen, I became pregnant.

My boyfriend's grandparents were raising him, and they were very religious. He made it clear that there was no way he would tell them what happened. I was too immature to make my own decision or even know who I was at that time. I was also terrified of what my mother would say or do, and I was not willing to confess the reality of my emotional state. My boyfriend found an advertisement in the local newspaper for a doctor in our town who performed abortions at his practice, and he made the appointment. It's been many years since that day in 1986, but certain events will never leave my memory.

When I walked into the office to check in, the nurse was kind until she saw the reason for my appointment. Her demeanor changed quickly to a hateful, judgmental attitude; remember, this was an obstetrics and gynecology (OBGYN) practice.

My boyfriend sat in the waiting room while the nurse escorted me to a back room on the opposite side of the building from the standard exam rooms. The doctor explained the procedure and began.

If you can believe the irony, he was equally judgmental as the nurse and, honestly, downright verbally abusive. If I made any sound in response to pain or discomfort, he would make hateful comments indicating that I deserved it. Several times, he yelled at me and made obscene, unrepeatable comments along the lines of, "Good, maybe this will teach you a lesson." I'm putting it much nicer than what he actually said. There were also many curse words and names thrown at me. It was such an awful, shameful experience that I will never forget.

Afterward, I went to a friend's house and spent the night recovering. A few days later, I began to feel sick, nauseous, and fevered. I had to go back to see the same doctor again. When he examined me, he found that, apparently, he had missed some parts of the baby the first time. He started cursing and kicking things around the room in anger. When his tantrum was over, he redid the procedure to vacuum out the parts he missed.

I did my best to block out what happened during the procedure. I could not tell any of my family members because that was why I did it in the first place, right? I felt so ashamed. I did not want anyone to know what I had done. Within the year, I left behind everyone and everything I knew and moved halfway across the country with a friend and her family.

It's hard to describe what happened to me after the abortion. I was so ashamed of myself that when I met men who were worth my time, I was uncomfortable with them and dumped them immediately. In college, I met a great man who would have been good for me, but I sabotaged the relationship because I did not believe I deserved him. He was the very last "good guy" I dated.

There was a very self-destructive stronghold in me; I became sexually promiscuous and abused alcohol. I had no idea why I was doing what I was doing, but still, I kept doing it. I was very depressed but unaware why I was depressed. There was a deep cry in my heart for something—self-worth, maybe. I felt so numb, without any joy or pleasure in anything I was doing, but I insisted on staying in that cycle of self-destruction.

Eventually, I got married to break the cycle! Of course, I was in no state to attract marriage material, so that was a tragic and wounding relationship that lasted about six years.

It wasn't until my early thirties, when I wanted a child, that God began to work in me to face the reality of what I had done. I was afraid I would not be able to get pregnant. I feared God would punish me by not allowing me to have a child. But that is not who He is. He blessed me with a pregnancy within a few months.

I had such a deep connection with my son from the womb. Sensing the presence of the blessing that was growing inside me, I began the process of grieving the child I had aborted. Being pregnant was one of the greatest joys of my life; I genuinely loved it. Then, after my son's birth, I had another unplanned pregnancy, but she died in utero at fourteen weeks. Grieving her loss solidified my knowledge of the true value of human life.

Looking back now, I see that God was with me all along. It's hard to imagine that in my pain, abuse, trauma, drunkenness, sexual impurity, and even in my deepest state of sinfulness, He was still with me. But it's true. All along, He was waiting for me to turn toward Him and open my heart to Him. I just could not see the forest for the trees. It's not because I am such a great weapon in the hands of God. It has nothing to do with me. It's because that is who He is; Jesus is love Himself. He CHOSE me even before the foundation of the world. What? If He chose me, then He must have known me! In love, He predestined me to be adopted as His! What? The God of the universe chose to adopt me! By Jesus's blood,

I have been redeemed and forgiven for my wrongs. This is what enabled me to forgive myself.

But it does not stop there; I also have an inheritance in Christ Jesus! (See Ephesians 1:4-11 [NIV].) Because I am His inheritance, He has cleansed and healed more pain, trauma, and unforgiveness than I can put into words.

My son is nineteen years old as I write this. God used him to heal so much in me and change the course of my life. Children truly are a blessing from God. What a legacy my son has been in my life!

I am also constantly aware that I have two daughters who, together, are waiting for me in Heaven. Their names are Lydia Caroline (aborted in 1986) and Olivia Grace (miscarried at fourteen weeks). This testimony is for Lydia. You are never forgotten, my love. You are worthy of acknowledgment. You were always worthy of life and our love. Praise God that I will see you both, face-to-face, someday.

I want to take this opportunity to call out the wickedness that resides in the industry of abortion. My story of verbal abuse and the shame heaped on me during my procedure is not uncommon in our society.

The point is this: when the human heart decides that ending the life of a God-given blessing could be a money-making business, there cannot be professional, honest, loving "health care." The two are at war with one another. For an entire industry (or just one doctor in my case) to set its mind against God's ordained creation, it must have already opened the door for wickedness. To say it is caring is a lie from the pit of hell; the entire concept of abortion is all one big lie from the enemy.

Jacquie's Story

I was born the sixth of seven children to a family in New Orleans. My father was a genius and a hard worker. He had great difficulty expressing emotions due to what we now suspect was Asperger's Syndrome. My mother was orphaned at age four and grew up in foster care. As a couple, they were not prepared for the challenges of a big family. In short, they did the best they could, but our home was not a happy place.

I had a friend down the street who had the nicest mom ever, Ma Blouin. I spent a lot of time there. I also loved school, where all the adults were patient and nice. In fifth grade, I was selected for a pilot program for gifted and talented students. It was incredible.

As a child, I grew up knowing I needed to pay my own way, so I was always interested in earning money. I worked odd jobs, like babysitting and yard work.

At sixteen, I drove to southern Florida to live with my older sister. I worked at a donut shop until I returned to Louisiana for my sophomore year of high school. The Gifted & Talented Program was not available in my high school, and I was not interested in the clubs, so I focused strictly on academics and was an honor roll student. I decided that going to community college would make working full-time easier. Against the counselor's advice, I took the General Educational Development (GED) test and drove back to Florida. I was just shy of seventeen when I started at Broward Community College.

My adolescence had been atypical and filled with lots of responsibilities, but it all seemed normal to me. I was happy. Life was full and good. I was busy, working two jobs and attending community college full-time. And I met Jesus!

It was the best thing that had ever happened to me. I set about trying to learn about God and His Word and grow in my faith. I went to Evangelism Explosion Coral Ridge Ministries in Fort Lauderdale. I had no idea what I was doing, and I was by far the youngest member of the Single Element in Action class at Coral Ridge. Regardless, I became friends with Maxx, who was probably in his seventies. He spoke blessings over my life and wrote beautiful letters of encouragement to me. I had never experienced that before. I was also actively involved in social activities, played on the co-ed softball team, and occasionally went scuba diving.

At eighteen, I got a job working third shift as a telephone rep for American Express. I earned more money than my other two jobs combined, received insurance, a 401(k) match, and college reimbursement. It was an outstanding year.

Then, in 1984, at nineteen, I was raped. I had gone to watch fireworks at the beach with an acquaintance I knew from the gym. I didn't sense any danger. I didn't see it coming or realize what was going to happen until that moment....

I was hours late to meet my sister to drive home for our brother's wedding. That was not like me. My sister wanted an explanation, but I didn't tell her anything.

While in Louisiana for the wedding, I was very sick and had streams of blood in my urine. But I refused to go to the doctor. When I returned to Florida, I did not attend the B summer semester classes as planned—again, not like me.

Then, terrible nightmares forced me to acknowledge what had happened. I began to stutter randomly, one eye shook uncontrollably, and I could not sleep. Out of desperation, I went to the doctor. I didn't even know a pregnancy test had been done. When the doctor called, he was choked up when he told me I was pregnant.

I was shocked and confused; however, I instantly loved my child. I was a biology major, so I knew she already had all the genetic code that determined her sex, her hair color, body type, etc. I thought of her as a tiny separate person with her whole future ahead of her. In all of my confusion, one thing was clear: I fiercely wanted to protect her.

I struggled with mental health issues. I was perpetually terrified, even when there was no apparent reason to be afraid. Invasive thoughts of the rape flooded every moment when my mind wasn't occupied, such as simply stopping at a red light, walking into work, and doing laundry.

I was also tortured in my sleep. I experienced a wide range of nightmares where the rapist was even in places I had not been since I was a child—the State Capital, the bus area at my middle school, etc. I could not control myself. My eye continued to shake, I randomly stuttered, and at times, I was so distraught that I'd hyperventilate. I simply could not control my body's reaction.

I tried not to act on my fearful thoughts and would make myself carry on with daily living. Sometimes, it worked; sometimes, it did not. Once, I was in the Winn-Dixie parking lot when I was overwhelmed with fear of the rapist. I went through the logic: I needed groceries, it was the middle of the day... but I was terrified. So, I ran into the store like someone was chasing me.

I bargained with myself that, if the invasive thoughts didn't get better, I would take my own life after I gave birth. I didn't really want to die; I just needed the perpetual fears and invasive thoughts to stop.

I continued to do well at work. My coworker, Marilyn, and I worked closely together as third-shift telephone representatives for American Express. Years before, Marilyn had been a nun. I was raised Catholic, so we shared our faith. I told Marilyn about the rape early in my pregnancy. Marilyn's sea blue eyes were filled with tears. I knew her heart for me. She had an inside view of how I had struggled, and she knew I needed the torment to stop.

"You have been through so much. God will understand," she told me.

I simply said, "This baby is the good part." Nothing else was said. Sometimes, when we speak the most truth, we sound like kindergarteners.

I took care of myself so I could take care of my baby. My baby gave me hope. I often thought about her future. I had a choice. I could place my child for adoption and carry on with my original plans, or I could be a parent.

Over time, my mental health improved somewhat, but it would wax and wane. Without making any contact with an agency, I privately considered adoption for the first few months. Then, I decided to be a parent. I would be Lauren Elizabeth's mom.

Even after giving birth, I was terrified of the rapist. There were times when I thought he was in the parking lot at work. My tires were slashed in the parking lot of my apartment. There was banging on my apartment door in the middle of the night. I didn't feel safe. Then, it happened. I saw the rapist watching me from behind a rack of clothing at a store. I knew right then that I had to leave Florida.

I briefly spoke with one person in human resources at American Express. I was a good employee, but as a twenty-year-old with an infant, I was an unlikely candidate for transfer. However, a few weeks later, movers arrived and put everything I owned, including my little Toyota Tercel, into a truck. I flew to Greensboro, North Carolina with Lauren. We stayed at a hotel downtown for a few weeks until we got settled in an apartment. I was Badge 20 at the North Carolina Regional Operating Center (NROC). It would eventually become one of the largest employers in Greensboro. When I look back, I know only God could have made that transfer possible.

I loved North Carolina! I marveled at the hiking trails at Hanging Rock, the beauty of the trees, and the wonderful people. I wanted to protect Lauren's privacy, so I told virtually no one about the rape conception. When asked about Lauren's father, I did not explain and just said I was single.

The first Sunday in North Carolina, I met a couple at church who became Lauren's godparents.

I wanted Lauren to grow up in a neighborhood. As a part of the relocation package, American Express paid closing costs. I used my 401(k) savings to buy a house. Our time there was filled with the joys of Lauren's young childhood. Our house was the neighborhood hangout for kids and the place for Easter egg hunts and big birthday parties. Lauren loved pets. She had a lop-eared rabbit, a guinea pig, a gerbil, and a dog. Life was good.

Fast forward to 2011. Lauren had just turned twenty-six and was about to be married. I knew she had become very interested in her biological father, so I googled the rapist's name. A series of newspaper articles from 1999 listed on the screen: "Victims of Rape Asked to Speak Up," "Paramedics Were Aware of Suspect's Behavior," and "Reports Show Trail of Charges." Then I knew. I wondered, all those years, if I really needed to leave Florida?—Perhaps, I had uprooted my life without any real threat. But my mental health issues had been real. I knew then that I was only one of his survivors. I called the district attorney and agreed to testify if, or when, they attempted to prosecute.

Shortly after, Lauren asked me to meet her at her favorite breakfast spot, International House of Pancakes (IHOP). I was shocked when Lauren pressed me for information. Her much younger brother had apparently overheard some of my conversations, but he didn't have any real information. Lauren bluntly stated, "I deserve the right to my history." I thought for a moment and agreed. I reluctantly told Lauren what I had found and that I had agreed to testify if needed. Lauren immediately volunteered to provide her DNA.

Lauren began researching and discovered that she has five half-siblings, all from different mothers. She has a brother who is five months older. The rapist's girlfriend was pregnant when he raped me. That mom called me. Although he had violently abused her, and that is why they didn't get married, she was shocked to learn of the rape.

Later, Lauren met a few of her siblings at Disney. She felt conflicted but still wanted to meet her biological father. However, before she arranged a meeting, he died unexpectedly. When I learned of the rapist's death, I was flooded with mixed feelings. I was immediately relieved that Florida was a safer place. It had been many years, and I had experienced healing. I felt safer. But I was also angry that I would not be able to testify against him. I had lost the opportunity to stand up to him. On the other hand, that chapter was finally over.

A few years ago, at fifty-seven, I felt led to join a new Sanctity of Life group at our church. Lauren was married, had a different last name, and lived a few hours away. I learned she spoke freely about her rape conception. So, after so many years, I began to tell my story. I am the woman for whom so many, even some pro-life people, want an exception to laws concerning abortion. I want to say some simple truths, MY truths. Babies are babies, no matter how they are conceived. And babies are the good part. I am filled with gratitude for Lauren. She was the unexpected gift I didn't know I wanted. Her life gave me hope and motivated me to do things I would not have done otherwise. Her life changed my life.

Looking back, I am so grateful that I protected myself from what I consider the tragedy of abortion. I feel fortunate. I had a God-given, fierce love and desire to protect my baby from the moment I knew of her. My baby's life was so precious that it motivated me to carry on when I was in the depths of despair. It shielded me from the deception that abortion would reset my life. As challenging as my unexpected pregnancy was, I am filled with gratitude for the opportunity to be my daughter's mom. **She was the good part.**

Unplanned pregnancies can be complicated. The circumstances of some unplanned pregnancies are heartbreaking. New plans have to be made. Hold on to what you know is true. Life is precious. There are choices. Moms can parent or place their babies for adoption. We need to love them both because there is hope in life.

RESOURCES

I want to hear from you! Please get in touch with me through my website (www.KellyProehl.com) and share your story. I'd love to pray for you also.

Below are some additional resources:

- 24/7 National Abortion Recovery Helpline: H3helpline (866) 721-7881 or online at www.h3helpline.org
- https://AbortionHealing.org/
- *Soul Care* by Dr. Rob Reimer
- *Jesus In Me: Experiencing the Holy Spirit as a Constant Companion* by Anne Graham Lotz
- www.EmbraceGrace.com
- Abortion Recovery Bible studies:
  - A Virtual Interactive Abortion Recovery Small Group: An Even Place / http://www.anevenplace.com/
  - *Surrendering the Secret* by Patricia Layton
  - *Forgiven and Set Free* by Linda Cochrane

- *"Healing a Father's Heart: A Post-Abortion Bible Study for Men"* by Linda Cochrane and Kathy Jones
- Abortion Recovery Retreats:
  - Deeper Still (men and women)
  - https://deeperstill.org/
  - Rachel's Vineyard (men and women) / https://www.rachelsvineyard.org/
  - Reassemble Life (women, men, and couples) / https://www.reassemblelife.com
  - She Found His Grace (online mentoring) / https://www.shefoundhisgrace.org/

Direct Bible-Related Resources:

- The Holy Bible
- Bible Study Fellowship / www.BSFInternational.org / an interdenominational, in-depth Bible study for men, women, teens, and children
- "Daily Audio Bible" Free App (DAB) / the Bible-in-a-year on audio for adults and kids (also in other languages)

NOTES

I. John Piper. "God Wrote a Book: Where Else Will We Run?" June 9, 2015. *Desiring God, YouTube*, 5:03.

II. Kristin McLelland, *The Gospel on the Ground* (LifeWay Press, May 2, 2022).

III. Paula Rinehart, *Sex and the Soul of a Woman* (Zondervan, Feb. 17, 2004).

IV. Ibid.

V. Christine Caine, Twitter post, August 30, 2017.

VI. Patricia Layton, *Surrendering the Secret: Healing the Heartbreak of Abortion* (LifeWay Press, 2008).

VII. Jill Marquis, *Forgiven and Set Free: A Bible Study for Women Seeking Healing after Abortion.* (Baker Publishing, Sept. 6, 2022).

VIII. Ann Voskamp, *One Thousand Gifts: A Dare to Live Fully Right Where You Are* (Thomas Nelson, Jan. 25, 2011).

IX. C. S. Lewis, *Signature Classics from the Letters Collection* (HarperOne, Feb. 14, 2017).

X. Pastor Greg Laurie, *Forgiveness is not Optional* (thinke.org, July 1, 2025).

XI. David Van Biama, "Should All Be Forgiven?" *Time Magazine*, April 5, 1999.

XII. Lee Strobel, *The Case for Christ* (Zondervan, Sept. 6, 2016).

XIII. Lee Strobel, *Is God Real?* (Zondervan, Oct. 31, 2023).

XIV. C. S. Lewis, *Surprised by Joy: The Shape of My Early Life* (Houghton, Mifflin, Harcourt).

XV. Josh McDowell and Sean McDowell, PhD, *Evidence that Demands a Verdict* (Authentic Media, Jan. 15, 2018).

XVI. Dr. David Jeremiah, Divine Resident—the Holy Spirit, Shadow Mountain Community Church, shadowmountain.org.

XVII. Dr. Austin Rogers, *Ten Secrets for a Successful Family* (Crossway Books, Jan. 1, 1996).

XVIII. Dr. David Jeremiah, *Revealing the Mysteries of Heaven* (Turning Point, Jan. 1, 2017).

ABOUT THE AUTHOR

Kelly is a wife, mom, "Lolli", and entrepreneur. She has been fortunate to spend time with people all over the country while moving from state to state during her husband Ricky's lengthy NFL career. During this time of growth through multiple changes, she worked tirelessly to build two top leadership positions in her wellness business, gaining life experience from many angles. However, nothing has shaped Kelly more than the healing power of Jesus.

Kelly and Ricky chose to have an abortion the end of their senior year in college. After living with this secret in silence and shame for many years, Kelly found healing and peace through a relationship with the Lord. She now writes and speaks boldly about the freedom, joy, and abundant life available through the Healer, Jesus Christ. For almost three decades, Kelly has studied and applied biblical truth to her life, and helped others discover that there is a Healer who can restore even the deepest wounds, including the wound of abortion.

She is passionate about wellness in all aspects of life. She demonstrates this daily through her work with the non-profit she and Ricky co-founded, The Ricky Proehl P.O.W.E.R. of Play Foundation, that serves children in-need—meeting spiritual, emotional, and financial needs with compassion and purpose.

Kelly and Ricky split their time between North Carolina and South Carolina, where she cherishes beach life, bike rides, sailing, writing, and time with family and friends. Kelly loves speaking at events to share the healing and mighty love of Jesus. Her memoir is a testament to God's relentless grace and a gift to anyone longing to live in soul-freedom from abortion—or any sin that entangles someone.